MORAL
RELATIVISM

MORAL
RELATIVISM

Steven Lukes

BIG IDEAS/SMALL BOOKS

PICADOR

New York

For Martin Hollis (1938–1998)
In this book our conversation continues.

CONTENTS

PREFACE

Many people, when they think about issues that seem to call for moral judgment, find themselves torn between two conflicting intuitions. One is the thought that there are actions and modes of behavior that are right and others that are wrong universally; and that people everywhere are harmed if they are mistreated in certain ways and if they lack, but could have access to, certain basic preconditions for living minimally well—food, shelter, and a range of resources, services, and opportunities. We may disagree about which ways they ought and ought not to behave, about how they should and should not be treated, and about which resources, services, and opportunities are, in this sense, universally basic. But we share the intuition that there are right answers to such moral questions. (Indeed, when we so disagree, we disagree about what the right answers are.) The other intuition is captured by the question Who are we to judge other cultures? Who are *we*, we may ask, to apply our standards to the adherents of other moral and religious systems? After all, they may not agree with us about what are right and wrong ways of behaving. They may not agree that what we take to be harmful is harmful. They may not agree that the preconditions we assume to be essential to every worthwhile human life are so, and they may deny that all human beings (for example, women) are entitled to have access to them.

The one thought leads us to make moral judgments; the other to abstain from doing so. The one presumes that there are moral absolutes; the other views such a claim as presumptuous. The first thought may derive from religious faith, from a belief in natural law, or from a rationalist view of progress; these days it is likely to be expressed in terms of human rights. The second thought leads, when developed, into what is widely called "moral relativism"—a bundle of ideas that in turn spring from two key thoughts: diversity and value conflict. Moral relativists are struck by what they take to be the diversity of morals across history and across the contemporary world. Anyone's moral views and practices are historically formed and local, and but for the accident of one's being born in a given time and place, these would have been other than they are. Furthermore, they see these views and practices, when they diverge, as rooted in irresolvable conflicts of underlying values. The confluence of these thoughts leads them to hold that moral judgments are relative to their time and place, so that they cannot be objectively justified and so cannot be absolute. So moral relativists believe that we cannot step outside our moral world, which is only one among others, and that our judgments of those inhabiting other such worlds can therefore have no special claim on them, and can only appear to them as ethnocentrism or moral imperialism on our part, or both.

There are four ways of responding to the issue as I have sketched it here. 1. One can espouse unqualified moral absolutism and deny that moral relativism has any plausibility. 2. One can espouse unqualified moral relativism and deny that moral absolutism has any plausibility. 3. One can view the suggested conflict between intuitions as unreal, either because I have mischaracterized what is at stake, or because it is deemed uninteresting or irrelevant. And 4—the argument I shall pursue for the rest of this book—one can address the conflict and ask: can it be resolved and, if so, how? In developing this argument, I hope, of course, to persuade adherents of (1) and (2) that they each face a genuinely plausible alternative, and adherents of (3) that the conflict in question is real, properly posed, interesting, and important.

Moral relativism is central, as we shall see, to some of the most divisive public issues of our times, where the idea, if not always the label, is repeatedly invoked. Is there a "clash of civilizations"? Are there distinctively Asian values? With growing mass immigration, moral relativism often inspires the policies and legal arguments of multiculturalism, in the name of *respecting* other communities and their traditions. But what does such respect require and what does it exclude? What does invoking the familiar slogan "It's their culture" permit? Moral relativism figures in debates about how to respond to Islamist terrorism and to religious extremism across the world. It often plays a part in identity politics, in confrontation with mainstream values, and in postcolonial discourse, reacting to the imperial hegemony of the West. It enters the politics of human rights and of humanitarian intervention. Are these just the latest form of cultural imperialism? By what right do we judge particular practices as barbaric? Who are the real barbarians?

RELATIVISM: COGNITIVE AND MORAL

There is *only* a perspective seeing, *only* a perspective
"*knowing.*"   NIETZSCHE[1]

Relativism is an inherently controversial topic. The very word inspires polemics that are sometimes passionate and often hostile. Relativism seems to be a threat to intellectual certainties, on the one hand, and to moral seriousness, on the other. Here are just two examples. Pope Benedict, on the eve of his election, proclaimed that we are "moving toward a dictatorship of relativism which does not recognize anything as for certain and which has as its highest goal one's own ego and one's own desires."[2] And in his best-selling book, *The Closing of the American Mind: How Higher Education Has Failed Democracy and Impoverished the Souls of Today's Students,* the late Allan Bloom wrote that "relativism has extinguished the real motive of education, the search for a good life."[3]

Both these statements suggest that what their authors call "relativism" has already secured wide appeal, and both focus on *moral* relativism, which certainly does seem plausible and attractive to many people, even if they don't use, or even reject, the label. What is it that causes those who denounce it such concern? In this book I shall try to clarify just what is at issue here. What exactly does a relativist assert, and what is distinctive about moral relativism? What is it about moral relativism that both attracts and repels? What is defensible in it and what should be rejected?

First we need to distinguish between relativism about knowledge, or cognitive relativism, and moral relativism, on which we will focus our attention.

Cognitive Relativism

Is what we can know determined by a world that is independent of us, or is it, in some sense, "up to us"? Immanuel Kant maintained that we cannot step outside the human standpoint—the circle of our own conceptions, theories, and reasonings—to a bare world as it is in itself, independent of them. Kant's philosophy was built on this unnerving thought, but Kant sought to defuse the threat. He used "we" inclusively to mean all of us human beings, together with any other being that humans could understand. So "we," in this inclusive sense, are all in the same boat with respect to knowledge and reason. Moreover, there is no cause for alarming uncertainty about what we can know and how we should reason. After all, the only knowledge available to us has to be intelligible to us. So it must be framed within the pregiven categories (such as space, time, persons, and objects in causal relations with one another) that shape our thinking and make it possible. And since we are rational persons, how we reason is not up to us but set by the requirements of Reason (with a capital R).

But Kant's reassurances were gradually swept away and the thought became more unnerving. Friederich Nietzsche made a first major breach by advancing what is sometimes called "perspectivism"—writing that there is "*only* a perspective seeing, *only* a perspective '*knowing*' "[4]— according to which what we know is guided, shaped, even constituted by our desires, our passions—in short, our interests. There is no "true world" that is really objective but unknown to us humans. There are indefinitely many possible perspectives from which knowledge is to be had, and there is no prospect of their being brought to converge within a true, comprehensive theory of the world.

This thought becomes fully relativist when the idea of perspectives is tied to particular groups within humanity. Now the idea is that potentially all our ideas and theories are to be seen as local cultural formations, rooted in and confined to particular times and places, and that there is no independent "truth of the matter" to decide among them. This may in turn suggest that we as human beings have no shared standards on the basis of which we can understand one other. Now there are multiple "we's," each with "our" own standards of truth, reasoning, and morality. The term *we* is no longer inclusive but contrastive: it picks out *us* as opposed to others. As this idea spreads, Bernard Williams writes,

> [m]oral claims, the humane disciplines of history and criticism, and natural science itself have come to seem to some critics not to command the reasonable assent of all human beings. They are seen rather as the products of groups within humanity expressing the perspectives of those groups. Some see the authority of supposedly rational discourse as itself barely authority, but rather a construct of social forces.
>
> In a further turn, reflections on this situation itself can lead to a relativism which steps back from all perspectives and sees them all at the same distance, all true, none true, each of them true for its own partisans.[5]

Not all relativists travel the full distance of this reckless and giddy journey. Those who do often insist on "the socially constructed and politically contested nature of facts, theory, practices and power."[6] The very phrase "social construction"—and, worse still, "the social construction of reality"—has, for a while, had an intoxicating effect on thinkers in various social scientific disciplines. The effect was not to *refute* social scientists' theories and explanations or to *unmask* ways in which their findings can serve socially or politically powerful interests, but rather to *undermine* the very idea that scientific explanations are superior to others. So, for example, an archaeologist working for the Zuni Indian tribe, who believe that their ancestors came from inside the earth into a world prepared for them by supernatural spirits, writes that science "is just one of many ways of knowing the world" and that the Zuni worldview is "just as valid as the archaeological viewpoint of what prehistory is about." Another archaeologist, Dr. Zimmerman of the University of Iowa, explicitly rejects "science as a privileged way of seeing the world."[7] And the anthropologist Renato Rosaldo views social scientists' claims to "*objectivity, neutrality* and *impartiality*" as "analytical postures developed during the colonial era" which "can no longer be sustained": they are "arguably neither more nor less valid than those of more engaged, yet equally perceptive, knowledgeable social actors."[8]

The way for such assertions was prepared by, among others, three thinkers, who raised questions about the objectivity of science itself in its very heartland, namely, natural science. One was Paul Feyerabend, self-described "epistemological anarchist," who famously wrote in

Against Method that "science is much closer to myth than a scientific philosophy is prepared to admit. It is one of the many forms of thought that have been developed by man, and not necessarily the best. It is conspicuous, noisy, and impudent, but it is inherently superior only for those who have already decided in favour of a certain ideology, or who have accepted it without ever having examined its advantages and its limits."[9] A second was his fellow historian-philosopher of science Thomas Kuhn, whose enormously influential book *The Structure of Scientific Revolutions*[10] challenged the standard textbook picture of scientific progress cumulatively evolving toward the truth, suggesting instead that science proceeds through a succession of "incommensurable" paradigms, seen as constellations of group commitments. And the third is Bruno Latour, who engaged in anthropological studies of scientists' "laboratory life," claiming, for example that "nature" can never explain how a scientific controversy gets settled and proclaiming that "[i]rrationality is always an accusation made by someone building a network over someone else who stands in the way."[11] No space here, it would seem, for the role of factual evidence or of reasoning in settling disputes or advancing scientific knowledge. (Interestingly, Kuhn never licensed and both Feyerabend and Latour subsequently distanced themselves from the extreme relativist conclusions others have drawn from their writings.[12])

The idea that facts, or indeed "reality," are socially constructed is an intoxicating mix of three distinct ideas, as Ian Hacking has made clear in his book *The Social Construction of What?*[13] Each of these ideas is heady enough, and the first step to sobriety is to consider the plausibility of each in particular cases. (There is a difference, after all, between claiming that, say, quarks are socially constructed and claiming that attention deficit disorder is.) The first is the idea of *contingency*: the thought that our explanatory theories could have been quite otherwise—so that, for example, there could have been an equally successful alternative physics in no sense equivalent to existing physics. The second is the idea of *nominalism*: the thought that our categories and classifications are not fixed by the structure of the world but by our linguistic conventions. And the third is the idea, sometimes called *externalism,* that we believe what we do, not because of the reasons that appear to justify what we believe, but because of factors such as the influence of the powerful or of social interests or of institutional imperatives or of social networks. This last idea lies at the origins of the discipline called "the sociology of knowledge."

The classic founders of that discipline were reluctant to travel any significant distance down the relativist road. So Marx and Engels and later Marxists never supposed that their knowledge of history and the dynamics of capitalism was merely "local knowledge." It was, they thought, scientifically warranted. Ideology, by contrast, was distorting and deceptive (as opposed to objective, truth-tracking) thinking, rooted in and serving class interests. Emile Durkheim, French founding father of sociology, and the Durkheimians likewise trusted the rules of sociological method to guide one to results warranted by adequate evidence and well-formed theories—including the result that cosmologies and ways of classifying the natural world reproduce features of the social structure and that our most basic categories are born out of social experience. Karl Mannheim, Hungarian founder of the sociology of knowledge, claimed that "the thought of all parties in all epochs is of an ideological character," but he nevertheless repudiated "the vague, ill-considered and sterile forms of relativism with regard to scientific knowledge"[14] and came to think that undistorted thought could be attained by "socially unattached intellectuals." As Robert Merton, the distinguished American sociologist, observed, Mannheim's view was that intellectuals "are the observers of the social universe who regard it, if not with detachment, at least with reliable insight, with a synthesizing eye"[15] (a view hard indeed to square with the unremitting partisanship of intellectuals in the political and ideological battles of our times).

Various influences from different quarters subsequently impelled thinkers to speed further and faster down the road. From linguistics and anthropology came the so-called Sapir-Whorf hypothesis, according to which "[w]e dissect nature along lines laid down by our native languages. . . . [T]he world is presented in a kaleidoscopic flux of impressions which has to be organized by our minds—and this means largely by the linguistic system in our minds."[16] So Sapir wrote: "The 'real world' is to a large extent unconsciously built upon the language habits of the group. The worlds in which different societies live are *distinct* worlds, not merely the same world with different labels attached. We see and hear and otherwise experience very largely as we do because the language habits of our community predispose certain choices of interpretation."[17]

From anthropology (about which much more in the

next chapter) came the notion of divergent cosmologies and ways of reasoning—a notion that has intrigued a succession of philosophers. So the French philosopher Lucien Lévy-Bruhl speculated that "the reality in which primitives move is itself mystical" and their reasoning "pre-logical."[18] Sir Edward Evans-Pritchard, the great Oxford anthropologist, in his study of Zande witchcraft, oracles, and magic, sought to scotch this idea, noting that tribal peoples, living close to the harsh realities of nature, cope and survive by observation, experiment, and reason and that their mystical thought and behavior is mainly restricted to ritual occasions. Evans-Pritchard contrasted mystical with commonsense and scientific notions and had no qualms about judging Zande witchcraft beliefs as mystical, unfalsifiable, and illogical. Magical beliefs formed a mutually supportive network riven with contradictions and so ordered that they never too crudely contradicted sensory experience.[19] The British philosopher of social science Peter Winch boldly contested Evans-Pritchard's assumption that in matters of witchcraft "the European is right and the Zande wrong": the Zande were not seeking "a quasi-scientific understanding of the world," and it was the European, "obsessed with pressing Zande thought where it would not naturally go—to a contradiction—who is guilty of misunderstanding, not the Zande." Winch drew from this critique the relativist-sounding conclusion that "standards of rationality in different societies do not always coincide" and that "what is real and what is unreal shows itself in the sense that language has."[20] In this Winch was deeply influenced by the philosopher Ludwig Wittgenstein, who had also reflected on anthropological examples, notably Sir James Frazer's classic *The Golden Bough* and, indeed, Evans-Pritchard's study. So, Wittgenstein asked in *On Certainty,* is it wrong for "primitives" to consult an oracle and be guided by it?: "If we call them 'wrong' aren't we using our language-game as a base from which to *combat* theirs?" But, Wittgenstein continues, aren't we offering them reasons?: "Certainly, but how far would they go? At the end of reasons comes *persuasion.* (Think what happens when missionaries convert natives)."[21] In a famous metaphor, Wittgenstein writes elsewhere that when I reach this point, justifications run out: "I have reached bedrock, and my spade is turned. Then I am inclined to say: 'This is simply what I do.'"[22]

This debate continues. Most recently, two anthropologists have fiercely disagreed over the question of whether or not the Hawaiians who killed Captain Cook believed he was the embodiment of one of their gods. Gananath Obeyesekere is sure they did not, because they are as rational as we are. He is concerned to contest European "myth models" of the savage mind and opposes the idea of a "radical disjunction between the Western self and society and those of the pre-industrial world": what "links us as human beings to our common biological nature and to perceptual and conceptual mechanisms that are products thereof" is "practical rationality."[23] Plainly, he maintains, the Hawaiians were capable of making the discriminations necessary to prevent them from mistaking Cook for a god. Marshall Sahlins disagrees. He disputes the relevance to the Hawaiians' world of the appeal to what he calls "Western logic and commonsense." This "Western" viewpoint "constitutes experience in a culturally relative way" and misleads us when we try to make sense of alternative cosmologies, epistemologies, and systems of classification, which are "completely embedded in and mediated by the local cultural order" and at odds with scientific classifications that purport "to be determined by things in and of themselves." To apply our "commonsense bourgeois realism" to the interpretation of other cultures is "a kind of symbolic violence done to other times and other customs." And so Sahlins proclaims: "Different cultures, different rationalities."[24]

Another source of the relativist impulse is American pragmatism, which viewed language as a tool and linked the idea of truth to what is useful to us in satisfying our needs. Pragmatism (alongside Wittgenstein) powerfully influenced the philosopher Richard Rorty, who sped down the relativist road with scarcely a glance behind. These influences are readily apparent in this much-quoted passage from Rorty. It is, he suggests, "pointless to ask whether there really are mountains or whether it is merely convenient for us to talk about mountains," for "given that it pays to talk about mountains, as it certainly does, one of the obvious truths about mountains is that they were here before we talked about them. If you do not believe that, you probably do not know how to play the language games that employ the word 'mountain.' But the utility of those language games has nothing to do with the question of whether Reality as It Is In Itself, apart from the way in which it is handy for human beings to describe it, has mountains in it."[25] Rorty argued for abandoning the idea that we use language to *represent* the world and that truth registers a correspondence between what we say and how the world is. In consequence, we should abandon the whole vocabulary of *truth, objec-*

tivity, rationality, and so on and replace it with talk of *justification* to and *solidarity* with relevant others. Knowledge is not an accurate representation of "reality." Rather it is a belief that is justified to others and thus relative to the "grid" or framework that happens to prevail at any given time and place to determine what counts as relevant evidence. When Galileo defended the Copernican theory, on the basis of observations made with his telescope, against Cardinal Bellarmine, who appealed to the scriptural description of the fabric of the heavens, Galileo did not win the argument because his account was more "objective" and "rational," or because the evidence compelled it, and certainly not because it was true. He won because his version of the movements of the planets was relative to one of the "educational and institutional patterns of the day," namely, the pattern whose "rhetoric has formed the culture of Europe" and "made us what we are today."[26] In short, Galileo won because he played the game that won the day.

Rorty's skepticism about the basis for scientific claims to objectivity and his focus on the "rhetoric" of science points to a final major source fueling contemporary relativism: that is, various contributions to the history and sociology of science itself. As I have indicated above, a key text here was Thomas Kuhn's *The Structure of Scientific Revolutions,* in which Copernicus also plays a significant role by exemplifying the replacement of one "paradigm" by another. Kuhn's claim is that "Copernicus' innovation was not simply to move the earth. Rather it was a whole new way of regarding the problems of physics and astronomy, one that necessarily changed the meaning of both 'earth' and 'motion.'"[27] This illustrates

what Kuhn called the "incommensurability" of competing paradigms and led him to the striking conclusion
that "the proponents of competing paradigms practice
their trades in different worlds."[28] The transition across
incommensurable paradigms is not "forced by logic and
neutral experience" but consists in a "transfer of allegiance" by individual scientists that can occur "for all
sorts of reasons," some of which "lie outside the apparent sphere of science entirely," such as "idiosyncrasies
or autobiography or personality" and even "the nationality or the prior reputation of the innovator and his
teachers."[29]

This last suggestion—that scientists can be motivated
in their work by social factors external to science—was
the guiding idea of the so-called strong program in the
sociology of science. That program was "strong" because it suggested that such factors are what counts in
explaining what scientists accept as good or successful
science: it focused exclusively on the social determinants of scientific and even mathematical thought, and
its standard-bearers forthrightly proclaimed their adher-
ence to relativism. It is relativism's opponents, they
charged, "who grant certain forms of knowledge a privileged status, who pose the real threat to a scientific understanding of knowledge and cognition."[30] Knowledge,
in their account, is "any collectively accepted system of
beliefs," and the task is to explain the causes of that acceptance, "regardless of whether the beliefs are true or
the inferences rational"—by which, as relativists, they
mean "without regard to the status of the belief as it is
judged and evaluated by the sociologist's own standards."
Faced with a belief whose acceptance is to be explained,

the sociologist of scientific knowledge asks questions such as these: "[Is it] part of the routine and technical competences handed down from generation to generation? Is it enjoined by the authorities of the society? Is it transmitted by established institutions of socialization or supported by accepted agencies of social control? Is it bound up with patterns of vested interest? Does it have a role in furthering shared goals, whether political or technical, or both?"[31]

For instance, according to one well-known study, a seventeenth-century scientific controversy between William Boyle and Thomas Hobbes, in which Hobbes was soundly defeated mathematically, is presented as "an issue of the security of certain social boundaries and the interests they expressed," and the authors draw the general conclusion that, in view of "the conventional and artificial status of our forms of knowing," it is "ourselves and not reality that is responsible for what we know."[32] Indeed, "the compelling character of logic," authors of this school claim, "such as it is, derives from certain narrowly defined purposes and from custom and institutionalized usage." Its authority is "moral and social" and "the credibility of logical conventions" is "of an entirely local character."[33]

Arguments such as these always encountered resistance and eventually led to the heated "science wars" of the 1990s, in which the "realist" view that there can be objective scientific knowledge seemed to be challenged by a wide range of thinkers in various fields—cultural studies, cultural anthropology, feminist studies, media studies, comparative literature, and science and technology studies—all influenced by what is broadly labeled "postmodernist" thinking. Scientists rebelled at the idea of being viewed anthropologically as a tribe. They also balked at the suggestion that social factors—such as gender, sexual orientation, race and class, authority structures, peer-group acceptance, competition for prestige and funding, and "boundary work" to demarcate what is seen as scientific from what is not—were relevant to the explanation of what counts as scientific knowledge. These battles, in which each side correctly accused the other of misunderstanding, ignorance, and caricature, were not, however, just an academic squabble in which scientists confronted humanists and social scientists. They had a bearing on the contemporary rise of so-called creationist science and the claims of "intelligent design," and on doubts about the scientific claims of global warming. As Latour remarked, "dangerous extremists are using the very same argument of social construction to destroy hard-won evidence that could save our lives."[34] The postmodernist critique could lend support to wider challenges to scientific authority, challenges that neither side in the science wars was disposed to endorse.

From the beginning, relativist ideas about knowledge have met with two kinds of resistance. One is at the level of philosophical argument, into which we will not enter here. There is an abundant philosophical literature aimed at refuting relativist arguments, in various ways: by showing them to be self-refuting (why is your argument for relativism not itself relative?); by contesting particular positions, distinguishing tenable claims from untenable conclusions that they supposedly entail; and by arguing directly for our capacity to arrive at beliefs about how the world is that are objectively reasonable, binding on anyone capable of appreciating the relevant evidence, regardless of their social or cultural perspective.[35]

The other way of resistance is, so to speak, existential or experiential. It derives from the certainty, which is everywhere apparent, that, to use the Czech-British anthropologist-philosopher Ernest Gellner's graphic phrase, a "Big Ditch" divides the modern from the premodern world. The Big Ditch for Gellner refers to "the idea that a great discontinuity has occurred in the life of mankind, the view that a form of knowledge exists which surpasses all others" in cognitive power.[36] No one *really* doubts that science yields objective knowledge that enables us to predict and control our environment and that there has been massive scientific and technological progress, and no one *really* supposes that judgments of the cognitive superiority of later over earlier phases of science or of scientific over prescientific modes of thought are merely prejudices relative to "our" local conceptual or explanatory scheme. People across the world live many-layered lives that can combine magic, religion, and science in countless ways, but no longer in ways that preclude acceptance of the cumulating cognitive power of science. When people are ill, they can believe in miracles, prayer, and surgery. Creationists and religious fundamentalists take flu vaccines whose development presupposes the truth of Darwinism, fly in airplanes, and surf the Web on computers. Members of tribes who consult witch doctors seek cures in local hospitals when they can; and although countless people in modern societies hold innumerable weird and apparently irrational beliefs, they do so against the massive background of science-compatible common sense. Those who most loudly proclaim their antimodernism never reject the whole package. Anti-modernism is a modernist stance; there is no route back from modernity. Therefore, all the arguments for cognitive relativism that we have been considering so far amount to interesting challenges, not a seriously disturbing threat, to confidence in science. Cognitive relativism can only be tangential to the way we live our lives. Its proponents are responding to an academic and not an existential question.

Moral Relativism

It is different with moral relativism—which is why many of those who are firm and confident in their dismissal of cognitive relativism are less firm and confident when it comes to moral relativism, and many even reject the former and embrace the latter. For instance, Ernest Gellner wrote: "I am not sure whether indeed we possess morality beyond culture, but I am absolutely certain that we do indeed possess knowledge beyond both culture and morality."[37] For what David Hume called our "natural belief" keeps the threat of cognitive relativism at bay. Virtually no one really doubts that science progresses toward an ever truer picture of the world and that its methods generally yield explanations that, while always fallible and revisable, are capable of being absolutely or objectively true, determinable by the facts of the matter and the way the world is, and not dependent on the idiosyncrasies of our particular, local worldview. Here, when divergent theories obtain, we confidently expect them to converge on ever more veridical accounts of how the world works. Some may have less confident expectations of the *social* sciences, or of some of its departments, but only because they contrast these, on various grounds, with what is surer, the soft or softer with the hard. Although the rest of us take their results on trust and accept their authority, we know that the institutions within which scientists work, the professional culture they internalize, and the methods they employ enable scientists to track the truth.

In matters of morality, there is no longer such a sense of security. As Bernard Williams has put it, in "a scientific inquiry there should ideally be convergence on an answer, where the best explanation of the convergence involves the idea that the answer represents how things are; in the area of the ethical, at least at a high level of generality, there is no such coherent hope."[38] Of course, many people are certain of their moral views and judgments, but they know that many others, no less certain, have different views and make different judgments, and both groups know that many others lack their very certainty.

For these reasons we think differently about scientific and moral "truth." We distinguish between the truths delivered and deliverable by science and what are claimed or proclaimed to be truths of morality. And the thought that the latter might be *relative* or *local* is disturbing, as the American moral philosopher Thomas Scanlon has suggested, for three reasons. The first, and weakest, is that if people accept relativism, then they will lack the motivation to accept basic moral principles, even those forbidding such things as murder. But as Scanlon remarks, "I do not think that the spread of relativism would have much effect on the amount of violence in the world. The worst mass murderers have not been relativists, and many relativists accept, perhaps for varying reasons, the basic contents of ordinary morality."[39] The second reason is that relativism threatens to deprive us of moral confidence: of the sense that we are *right* to condemn the actions of wrongdoers and to think that their victims are entitled not to be wronged. And the third reason is that relativism removes the sense of *conflict* between apparently conflicting moral judgments by suggesting that since they are relative to different standards, they do not really conflict. When we are internally torn by conflicting moral intuitions, it really is hard to believe that our sense that there is a conflict is an illusion. (If anything in moral judgment is objective, it is surely the reality of such conflicts.) When we make a moral judgment, we appeal to a moral norm we take to have a particular authority—an authority that excludes others from having the same authority.

Moral relativism is the idea that the authority of moral norms is relative to time and place. *Norms* are rules that indicate which actions are required, prohibited, permitted, discouraged, and encouraged. Norms, we typically say, are external to individuals and "internalized" by individuals, and they guide individuals' behavior: they issue instructions to act or not to act. What distinguishes *moral* norms from others? As we shall see, this is disputable, and the dispute matters a great deal. Let us say, provisionally, that moral norms cover matters of importance in people's lives, where they are faced with distinguishing right from wrong. Moral norms are directed at promoting good and avoiding evil, at encouraging virtue and discouraging vice, at avoiding harm to others and promoting their well-being or welfare. In general, moral norms are concerned with the interests of others or the common interest rather than just with the individual's self-interest. They are also distinct from the rules of etiquette, law, and religion (though the conduct they require may overlap with what these require).

There are two ways of thinking about morality and moral norms. One can view them as an external observer, anthropologically or sociologically, seeing them as forming systems of morals or ethics, or codes of conduct, which vary from society to society, culture to culture, or even group to group. This is sometimes called a *descriptive* view of what morality is. In fact it involves both description and (causal) explanation: describing how moral norms function and explaining how they arise and how (by what mechanisms) they shape and influence people's thought and behavior. So we may speak of different "moralities"—the morality or morals or ethics of the ancient Greeks, say, or of Homeric warriors, or of Athenian or Spartan morals in particular. We may speak of the morality of the Renaissance courtier or of the American frontier or of the antebellum American South or of medieval samurai or of the Aztecs, or of Christian or Islamic or Hindu morality, or even of Puritan or Salafist or Brahmin morals. Viewed this way, moralities can vary widely, with regard both to their foundations and to their central concerns. They can be religious or pagan or atheistic. They can focus on military prowess or tribal feuding or reciprocal gift-giving or knightly chivalry or family honor or caste distinctions or sexual behavior or money-making or spiritual purity. Furthermore, they can embrace all kinds of practices, including slavery, racism, aggressive war-making, and ruthless oppression; and they need not exhibit impartiality or universalistic attitudes.

The second way of thinking about morality allows us, on the contrary, to view it as excluding and condemning practices such as these last as *immoral*. Here one is viewing morality not as an external observer but *practically*— from inside the practice of morality, as a moral agent or participant. One views it from a first-person rather than a third-person standpoint. In occupying this standpoint, I consider what I and others should or ought to do, what is right and wrong, what is obligatory and what is prohibited, what is good and bad, what is valuable and worthless, and so on. Moral norms now appear as principles and rules that I see as applicable to myself and anyone else similarly situated. In this view morality is single, not plural, though it may be internally complex and indeed contain conflicting principles. It is the one morality in terms of which I now make judgments (whether or not I follow its dictates). It applies to my conduct and practices and it enables me to judge those of others. From this internal standpoint, moral norms are justified and justifiable by reasons I find to be compelling, and so they are seen as a guide to conduct for myself and for all relevantly similar moral agents. We may think that many societies lack many of these norms and that many societies, even most, perhaps including our own, are to be judged in the light of them to be morally defective or degenerate or backward. The point is that in this view of morality—the agent's or participant's view—moral norms are appealed to and seen as binding on oneself and on all relevantly similar moral agents similarly situated, and so it is sometimes called the *normative* view of morality.

But now an intriguing question arises: *how far* does reasoning reach? Do the compelling reasons that justify the moral norms by which we judge apply to all persons everywhere and at all times? If they do not, should they?

Relativists answer these last two questions in the negative. Adherents of what we may call "standard" moral relativism hold that our reasoning, and thus the applicability of our moral norms, does not reach beyond the bounds of whatever our morality is relative to—our culture, say, or religion or language. Bernard Williams, who has no time for this doctrine, wants, however, to stake out a place for what he calls the "relativism of distance" in respect of societies that are sufficiently distant from us, not in space but in *time*. He argues that "the language of appraisal—good, bad, right, wrong, and so on" is inappropriate when we are considering, say, "the life of a Bronze Age chief or a medieval samurai," for these embody outlooks with which we are in merely "notional," not "real," confrontation. They are "not real options for us: there is no way of living them."[40] One can, writes Williams, "imagine oneself as Kant at the Court of King Arthur, disapproving of its injustices, but exactly what grip does this get on one's ethical or political thought?"[41] On the other hand, today "all confrontations between cultures must be real confrontations,"[42] since other cultures are "within our causal reach." After colonialism, when confronted "with a hierarchical society . . . , we cannot just count them as them and us as us: we may well have reason to count its members as already some of 'us.' "[43]

Thoroughgoing antirelativists, by contrast, hold our reasoning to be universal in scope, reaching across space and time. Our judgments and principles apply to all relevantly similar moral agents. But antirelativists and relativists will differ about what makes them relevantly similar. From within the normative standpoint, antirelativists will answer: their *common humanity*—the inclusive rather than the contrastive "us." These days they will speak the language of human rights. Relativists of the standard variety are or should be wary of such talk, while antirelativists like Williams, who want to keep a place for relativism regarding societies sufficiently distant in time, will confine such talk to the modern world.

Of course, as those taking the descriptive view of morality readily observe, there is considerable disagreement among moral agents or participants, including moral philosophers, as to which *are* the rationally justifiable and applicable moral rules and principles. Anthropologists, as Mary Douglas observes, "record many diverse social forms each venerating its particular idea of justice."[44] There is, it is true, very general agreement that certain sorts of actions, such as killing, deception, and breaking promises, are to be prohibited and that others, exhibiting a sense of fairness and loyalty and enhancing cooperation, are to be encouraged. But divergences set in once you ask under what conditions and in relation to whom these actions are to be respectively prohibited and permitted, and on what grounds. So, for instance, Kantians, utilitarians, believers in Natural Law, contractarians, perfectionists, liberals, and communitarians, not to mention adherents of different religions and of none, will give different accounts of the bases and content of moral norms. What is agreed by all those taking the internal normative view, however, is that moral norms are based on compelling reasons and binding on all who are relevantly similar and similarly situated.

Moral relativists begin from the observer's standpoint, adopting the descriptive view of morality, observing that there is a diversity of morals. They are struck by what they see as the *fact* of moral diversity: by the observation that moral norms form systems of norms, or moral codes, which differ from one society or culture or group to another. This amounts to saying that there are divergent views about what constitutes good and evil, virtue and vice, harm and welfare, dignity and humiliation, and where individual and common interests lie. They are further struck by the thought that these divergences can be irreconcilable: that the moral disagreements revealed by these divergences may not be capable of being rationally resolved, that they can lead to incompatible judgments, even that they may be incommensurable, lacking a common moral framework or shared concepts and standards. Of course, some disagreements will be resolvable by clearing up vagueness or indeterminacy in how norms are expressed, and in some cases they will be due to factual disputes or logical errors. But moral relativists insist, against so-called moral objectivists or absolutists, that the disagreements that divide societies and cultures spring from irreconcilable moral outlooks. They will further insist that their view is only strengthened by the fact that the objectivists disagree among themselves about which objectivist theory is the right one and by the reasonable-seeming prediction that there is no prospect of that disagreement ever coming to an end.

From their observation of the fact of moral diversity

and their view that this diversity is irreconcilable, moral relativists take the crucial step that defines full-fledged moral relativism. They hold that if the internal, participant's normative view of morality is taken to be universally applicable, reaching across space and time, then it is untenable. There is, they claim, no unique viewpoint from which moral norms are rationally compelling and universally binding. They may say this because they hold that there is no point beyond a culture from which we can judge others in a way that is not relative to our own position. This was how the distinguished American anthropologist Clifford Geertz deviously defended relativism by criticizing "anti-relativism" for "placing morality beyond culture and knowledge beyond both."[45] And it was the no less distinguished French anthropologist Claude Lévi-Strauss's point when he compared cultures to moving trains, reminding us that "for a passenger sitting by the window of a train, the speed and length of other trains vary according to whether they move in the same direction or the opposite way. And every member of a culture is as closely linked to that culture as the imaginary passenger is to his train."[46] They may say, like the Finnish philosopher-sociologist Edward Westermarck, who propounded ethical relativism at the London School of Economics, that since "there are no moral truths it cannot be the object of a science of ethics to lay down rules for human conduct" and that "the moral consciousness is ultimately based on emotions, that the moral judgment lacks objective validity, that the moral values are not absolute but relative to the emotions they express."[47] Westermarck's view was that our moral intuitions are in fact emotional tendencies formulated as judgments, which are calculated to give moral values an objectivity they do not possess.

Moral relativists may say, with the cautious American philosopher Richard Brandt, while preserving "a healthy degree of skepticism about the conclusiveness of the inquiry," that different groups "sometimes make divergent appraisals" though they have identical beliefs about the facts.[48] They may agree with the more forthright Australian moral philosopher John Mackie, who thought that ethics is a matter of "inventing" right and wrong, that the radical differences in moral judgment that we observe "make it difficult to treat those judgments as apprehensions of objective truths."[49] The authority of moral norms comes, they may say, not from reason but from religious authority, say, or tradition or custom or convention, and its scope of application is local and time-bound. So we can only participate in morality understood in the descriptive sense—that is, in one morality or another—in *this* morality as opposed to *others*. In other words, the "first-person," practically oriented perspective of the moral agent has to be rethought and reformulated. Moral judgments are always to be understood and expressed in a relativistic manner. Moral principles are only properly expressed when a "relativizing clause" is appended to them. In short, our judgments about right and wrong are not, as we have supposed, unqualified and absolute, but relative to our society or culture, or whatever group turns out to be the source of our moral framework.

So, for example, Mary Douglas, the anthropologist, criticizes the political philosopher Brian Barry for arguing that justice rests on principle, not convention. When Barry claims that systematic group discrimination and economic and social privilege based on birth are, even if universally accepted in a given society, unjust, Douglas comments that he "is expressing the legitimating principles of the conventions created to maintain a particular set of institutions, to wit, those of Western industrial society. Yes, for us, who have internalized the justice of these institutions, such inequality is clearly unjust."[50] And when Barry insists that if "someone can read a history of European settlements in Australia and the Americas, or a history of negro slavery, without admitting that he is reading a history of monstrous injustice, I doubt that anything I can say is likely to convince him."[51] Douglas sees this as comparable to a theologian's justification of religious truth in mystic experience. The theologian too says, "[N]othing I say will convince him: the feeling is incommunicable." It is, she claims, very hard to defend a substantive principle of justice as universally right without "appeal to religion, intuitionism or innate ideas."[52]

This progression of thought is not, however, inexorable. You can accept descriptive relativism, acknowledging the diversity of morals in the descriptive sense—though, as we shall see in Chapter 3, this is no simple matter. You can then switch roles and, as a moral agent who participates in morality in the normative sense, view your moral principles as objective or absolute, and justified by reasons. But you will then have to take a view about moral pluralism—the alleged plurality of objectivist accounts of morals. You can deny such pluralism, as many do, holding that your morality is the

One True Morality, and that the others are in error. You might be what philosophers call a "moral realist" and hold to "the idea that moral questions have correct answers, that the correct answers are made correct by objective moral facts, that moral facts are determined by circumstances, and that, by engaging in moral argument, we can discover what these objective moral facts are."[53] Or else you can try to find a way to reconcile moral objectivity and moral pluralism.

I said that moral relativists start out from the observation of moral diversity: the alleged fact of moral diversity raises the question of moral relativism. But it is important now to qualify this by noting that their conclusion, just stated, though *motivated* by the alleged facts of moral diversity, does not depend on the *actual* existence of such diversity. This mistake is often made by those who wrongly suppose that if moral norms or practices were shown to be cultural universals, such as, say, the prohibition of incest, this would tell against the case for moral relativism. But as Cook observes, the relativist will reply as follows: "A principle that is found to be accepted in all cultures is just as relative as a principle that is accepted in some but not all cultures, for (1) those that are universally accepted still prescribe conduct for only the members of presently existing cultures, and (2) it would be absurd to think that if a new culture evolved tomorrow, it would be morally inferior if it did not incorporate those principles that are now universally accepted."[54] Indeed, theoretically, even if much or all of human morality turned out to be shared in common, there would still be the potentiality of diversity emerging, and that shared morality would, in the moral relativist view, be relative to all currently existing societies. All that moral relativism requires to get going is the postulate of actual or potential diversity or both. And the relativity of morals does not mean the absence of universal acceptance, but rather the denial of universal applicability.

Of course, moral relativists, in denying the rational basis and universal applicability of moral norms, are faced with the problem of accounting for their undoubted *authority*. For these norms confront us with demands and requirements. As Durkheim argued, they are "social facts"—external to and independent of us as individuals and exerting a constraining influence upon us. Why, after all, do we obey moral rules and conform to moral principles and feel guilt and shame when we deviate from them? Here, then, is an answer: the source of moral authority is *social*. Are "morals" the same as the customs or mores of a given society? William Graham Sumner, early American sociologist and author of *Folkways,* who coined the very word *ethnocentric,* wrote that " 'Immoral' never means anything but contrary to the mores of the time and place,"[55] and the cultural relativist anthropologist Ruth Benedict briskly remarked that "morality . . . is a convenient term for socially approved habits."[56] This answer, in one form or another, is, as we shall see in the next chapter, as old as the ancient Greeks and has continued to be advanced and disputed until today.

2

REASON, CUSTOM, AND NATURE

> ...we think that it is reason which is unhinged
> whenever custom is—and God knows how often
> unreasonably we do that!   MONTAIGNE[1]

Can we escape from custom through reason? Perhaps reasoning is just an activity governed by local customs or conventions, so that standards of rationality—what counts as a reason and what counts as a good reason— vary from society to society, culture to culture, institution to institution, group to group. Or does reasoning dictate its own norms, enabling us to stand back from, reflect upon, and either criticize or endorse our customs and the customs of others, and enabling them to do likewise?

Herodotus addressed this question in the form of a famous story that he took to vindicate a saying of the Greek poet Pindar: that "custom is lord of all." The story concerns Darius the Great, King of Persia, who

summoned the Greeks who were with him and asked them for what price they would eat their fathers' dead bodies. They answered that there was no price for which they would do it. Then Darius summoned those Indians who are called Callatiae, who eat their parents, and asked them (the Greeks being present and understanding through interpreters what was said) what would make them willing to burn their fathers at death. The Indians cried aloud, that he should not speak of so horrid an act. So firmly rooted are these beliefs; and it is, I think, rightly said in Pindar's poem that custom is lord of all.[2]

Herodotus comments that each nation is convinced that its own customs are "by far the best." Mary Midgley, who cites this story in her fine little book *Can't We Make Moral Judgments?*, makes the apt comment that in this story the Persian King appears "in the role of the detached, sophisticated, neutral observer above the dispute who understands other people's difficulties. He is the one who can see through superficial symbols to the reality behind them. The Persians, after all, neither burned their own dead nor ate them. They knew very well that they had solved the problem of disposal in the only *right* way, namely by putting corpses on high towers and letting the vultures eat them."[3]

Custom and the Cannibals

In the sixteenth century Michel de Montaigne took up this theme in several of his essays, notably those on custom and on the cannibals. Like Herodotus, he endorsed Pindar's saying about "custom's imperial sway," adding that "there is nothing that custom may not do and cannot do," for "there is no notion, however mad, which can occur to the imagination of men of which we do not meet an example in some public practice or other and which, as a consequence, is not propped up on its foundations by our discursive reason."[4] Notice that here reason is simply "propping up" what custom requires. Montaigne also writes of reason as a mere coloring—"a dye spread more or less equally through all the opinions and all the manners of us humans, which are infinite in matter and infinite in diversity."[5] Moreover, custom seems inescapable, for

> the principal activity of custom is so to seize us and to grip us in her claws that it is hardly in our power to struggle free and to come back into ourselves, where we can reason and argue about her ordinances. Since we suck them in with our mothers' milk and since the fate of the world is presented thus to our infant gaze, it seems to us that we were really born with the property of continuing to act that way. And as for those ideas which we find to be held in common and in high esteem about us, the seeds of which were planted in our souls by our forefathers, they appear to belong to our genus, to be natural. That is why we think that it is reason which is unhinged whenever custom is—and God knows how often unreasonably we do that![6]

And yet this last phrase suggests that Montaigne is appealing to what is "reasonable" and thus, as Tzvetan Todorov, Franco-Bulgarian author of *On Human Diversity,* puts it, using the instrument he has just declared unusable.[7] Montaigne goes on to recommend that it is better to subject custom to rational scrutiny, for a "man who wished to loose himself from the violent foregone conclusions of custom will find many things being accepted as being indubitably settled which have nothing to support them but the hoary whiskers and wrinkles of attendant usage: let him tear off that mask, bring matters back to truth and reason, and he will feel his judgment turned upside-down, yet restored by this to a much surer state."[8] Indeed, he advises that the wise man should withdraw his soul from the crowd, "maintaining its power and freedom freely to make judgments, whilst externally accepting all received forms and fashions."[9]

Plainly, Montaigne thought that reason could escape the grip of custom, even if only to restore it to a much surer state and enable a wise man to live well. And of course his very essay-writing was a wonderful example of reasoning—a custom he did much to inaugurate. In his essay on the cannibals he deployed it in addressing a question central to the debate over moral relativism, namely, Who are the real barbarians? In raising this question, Montaigne was engaging in a moral and social critique of the practices of his own society. This mode of argument was to recur across the entire period that stretched from the time of the first discoveries, in which he lived, to the heyday of modern anthropology— from the eighteenth century's "noble savage," Montesquieu's Persians and Diderot's Tahitians, to Margaret Mead's Samoans—during which descriptions of reported and imagined exotic cultural practices exercised a continuing fascination over the Western mind. Accounts of cannibalism, for the most part conjured and embellished, were emblematic of this continuing fascination.

Montaigne's picture of the cannibals is derived from the reports of a "simple, rough fellow" of his acquaintance who had voyaged to Brazil and from his own reading of classical literature. Montaigne declared himself saddened by the fact that "while judging correctly of their wrongdoings, we should be so blind to our own. I think there is more barbarity in eating a man alive than in eating him dead; more barbarity in lacerating by rack and torture a body still fully able to feel things, in roasting him little by little and having him bruised and bitten by pigs and dogs (as we have not only read about but seen in recent memory, not among enemies in antiquity but among our fellow citizens and neighbors—and, what is worse, in the name of duty and religion) than in roasting him and eating him after his death."[10] Thus "we can indeed call these folk barbarians by the rules of reason but not in comparison with ourselves, who surpass them in every kind of barbarism."[11] Montaigne goes on to extol the cannibals' virtues: their "resoluteness in battle and love for their wives"[12]; their "noble and magnanimous" warfare, which is not engaged in to conquer new lands, since "a bounteous Nature" accords them all they need; their polygamous marriages, in which, it appears, women encourage men's love and tenderness for other women as testimony to their husband's valor; and their poetry, which Montaigne declares reminiscent of ancient Greek love poems.[13]

Montaigne, in short, finds that "there is nothing savage or barbarous about those peoples, but that every man calls barbarous anything he is not accustomed to; it is indeed the case that we have no other criterion of truth or right reason than the example and form of the opinions and customs of our own country. There we always find the perfect religion, the perfect polity, the most developed and perfect way of doing anything!"[14] But, we may ask, has Montaigne really escaped the ethnocentrism he here condemns? Is his picture of the cannibals and their practices not a projection of his prejudices and ideals, which are rooted in his own time and place? As Todorov observes, "Bravery in warfare and polygamy, cannibalism, or poetry will be excused or offered as examples, not in terms of the ethics of the Other, but simply because these features are found among the Greeks, who embody Montaigne's personal ideal. "[15]

There are, then, three themes in play—and at war with one another—in these two essays of Montaigne. One is the idea of *cultural determinism*: we are in the grip of custom. The second is the idea that we can escape its grip by the use of our reason—even if for the conservatively inclined Montaigne this meant to endorse the customs and conventions of one's own society. And the third is the idea of external social criticism: we can judge those customs and conventions by comparing them with those of other cultures. But can we do this without our accounts of those cultures embodying our own values? Is our external critique not after all limited, even shaped, by our internal cultural starting point? Understanding other cultures, especially exotic cultures, means rendering their practices intelligible to us, but to do this we need to use analogies to render the unfamiliar familiar. In his book *Morality and Cultural Differences,* John W. Cook refers to this as "the projection error."[16] But to call this an error is to assume we can avoid it. The deeper question is: can we avoid doing this, and if we cannot, are we not then limited, even trapped, in our understanding and thus judgment of others, within our own cultural horizon? Let us call this *the projection problem*. We will examine this more closely in the next chapter.

Montaigne was not consistently a moral relativist,

though there are certainly relativist-sounding passages in his *Essays*: for example, "the best and most excellent polity for each nation is the one under which it has been sustained. Its form and its essential advantages depend upon custom,"[17] and "I know of no better school for forming our life than ceaselessly to set before it the variety found in so many other lives, concepts, and customs and to give it a taste of the perpetual diversity of the forms of human nature."[18] Todorov calls him an unwitting or unconscious universalist because, in adducing the practices of the cannibals in criticism of those of his countrymen, he was allegedly unaware of taking his own ideals as universally valid. (Could so supremely self-reflective a thinker really have been unaware of his own biases?) What is striking is that Montaigne's discussion of these issues foreshadows the debates over moral relativism that were to come. As we shall see, the themes on which he touched have been central to these debates. In this chapter we consider cultural determinism and the role of reason.

The Cultural Relativists

The theme of cultural determinism lay dormant in Western thought until taken up by the Italian philosopher-historian Giambattista Vico and by Johann Gottfried Herder[19] (of whom we will hear more in Chapter 4). It became central to the doctrine of cultural relativism propounded by the twentieth-century American anthropologists who followed in the wake of Franz Boas, notably Melville Herskovits and Ruth Benedict. One key claim was that morality was acquired through what they called "enculturative conditioning"—a phrase which, interestingly, suggests that learning a culture is all-pervasive, largely unconscious, and occurs independently of reasoning. As the philosopher Michele Moody-Adams astutely observes, this suggests that one is placed "beyond the reach of certain motivational principles" and so "presupposes cultural determinism."[20] Thus Herskovits wrote:

> Cultural relativism developed because the facts of difference . . . in moral systems, plus our knowledge of the mechanisms of cultural learning, forced the realization of the problem of finding valid cross-cultural norms. In every case where criteria to evaluate the ways of different peoples have been proposed, the question has at once posed itself: "Whose standards?" The force of the enculturative experience channels all judgments. In fact, the need for a cultural relativistic point of view has become apparent because of the realization that there is no way to play this game of making judgments across cultures except with loaded dice.[21]

Boas and his followers introduced a new way of conceiving of "culture" and cultural learning. One of their innovations was to see this as largely driven by emotion rather than reason. As another Boasian, Clyde Kluckholm put it, cultural learning involved the acquiring of sacred beliefs that are beyond criticism, so that "the person who suggests modification or abandonment must be punished," and to these beliefs "emotional loyalty continues in the face of reason because of the intimate conditionings of early childhood."[22] The other innovation was to see this process as largely unconscious. In Boas's view, according to Elvin Hatch, "customs are habitual patterns of thought and behavior (most of which we learn as children), and, once we acquire them they become 'automatic' and 'unreflective,' like the rules of grammar. . . . Boas' view of the unconscious seems to have been that of a bundle of discrete, learned patterns, including grammatical rules, mythical plots, modes of etiquette and principles of artistic design, among others . . . [and] in his view there is a general tendency for the mind to work towards some degree of consistency among the patterns it contains."[23]

Thus the Boasians viewed cultures holistically, so that any given custom or practice only becomes intelligible when seen within its total cultural context. Each society makes a selection in its cultural institutions from what Benedict called "a great arc" of human interests, and the selection determines its identity as a culture.[24] The cultural relativists broke with the method, typical of writers from Montaigne to Westermarck, of comparing a custom here to a custom there, and turned instead to the study of custom and morality as these appeared in the lifeways of particular societies, usually primitive, studied intensively by direct observation. Anthropologists came to think that the "rightness" of shockingly different practices could only be assessed within the context of a whole way of life. So it was no longer possible, in Robert Redfield's words,

> to stop with the assertion, "Those people think it right to kill their fathers, or practice cannibalism, or marry one's sister." Seen in its full context, there was much more to be said as to why these things were done and thought right and good. The Eskimo who walled up an aged parent in a

snow house and left him to die, did so because in their hard, migratory life the old person could no longer travel, endangered his close kinsmen by his presence, and perhaps himself endured an almost unbearable existence. Furthermore, good reporters of actual cases of these assisted suicides—for that they were, rather than homicides—show the tenderness, even the filial respect, with which the thing was done. Cannibalism, found to be not one custom but many different kinds of customs, showed in one of its forms, a ritual partaking of the flesh of a slain enemy into which entered, among other elements of feeling and belief, a respect for the valor, one might say the spiritual strength, of that enemy.[25]

Redfield's point was that to these anthropologists

the shock of the different began to disappear as it came to be understood that each traditional way of life was a somewhat coherent statement, in thought and action, of a good life. Seen in context, most customs then showed a reasonableness, a fitness with much of the life, that allowed the outsider more easily to understand and more reluctantly to condemn. At this point in the development of differences in group-ways the phrase "cultural relativism" came into use. The basic tenet of cultural relativism is the proposition that the rightness of what is done by another people follows from *their* view of things, not from ours.[26]

Relativism and Tolerance

The outlook of the cultural relativists was egalitarian. Boas himself was a German-Jewish immigrant with left-of-center politics, critical of Western colonialism and its Christianizing and civilizing mission; and the Boasians, who came to dominate the anthropological profession in the United States, were progressives who in the 1920s and '30s combated preferential immigration laws and racial segregation. They sought to unseat the hitherto prevalent assumption that one could rank societies and civilizations as more and less advanced, as higher and lower, as civilized and primitive (or barbarian or savage). There were, they claimed, no criteria transcending cultural boundaries. And so Ruth Benedict ended her immensely influential book *Patterns of Culture,* comparing the customs of three strikingly different American Indian societies, with the claim that, once cultural relativity is recognized and "embraced as customary belief," we shall arrive at "a more realistic social faith, accepting as grounds of hope and as new bases for tolerance the co-existing and equally valid patterns of life which mankind has created for itself from the raw materials of existence."[27] Moreover, as this quotation indicates, they concluded that their relativism implied *tolerance* of those patterns of life and practices. Thus Herskovits wrote that cultural relativism was a philosophy that stressed "the need for tolerance of conventions though they may differ from one's own."[28] Moreover, he was clear that this was not a unilateral principle applying only to us: tolerance was a universally applicable principle.

This conclusion faces three objections. First, Herskovits and Benedict were mistaken—cultural relativism does not imply tolerance. If all our moral judgments are culturally bounded, we can just as well be nationalists or racists as egalitarians. Mussolini declared himself a moral relativist,[29] and Maurice Barrès, fierce anti-Dreyfusard, could write, "Nationalism requires us to judge everything with respect to France."[30] Furthermore, as Todorov has observed, "an entirely consistent relativist may demand that all foreigners go home, so they can live surrounded by their own values."[31] Secondly, as many critics of cultural relativism have pointed out, there is a striking inconsistency in asserting the relativity of all moral principles and then proclaiming the moral principle of tolerance as a universal principle and moreover one backed by reasoning, indeed adducing the doctrine of cultural relativism as the reason for adopting it. And thirdly, the implication of cultural relativism is forbearance: that is, *abstinence* from (nonrelative) moral judgments or, as Redfield put it, *reluctance to condemn.* Tolerance, by contrast, *presupposes* such negative judgment or condemnation. To tolerate something or someone is to abstain from acting against what one finds unacceptable. One exhibits tolerance by condemning but not intervening (and from a position of power: we do not speak of the weak tolerating the strong). If one approves of or is indifferent to something or someone, then "toleration" is not at issue. So by claiming that their relativism led to an attitude of *tolerance* the Boasians were drawing an invalid inference and being inconsistent, and they were misusing the term *tolerance.* What they meant, in misleadingly advocating tolerance, was to urge the according of equal *respect* by abstaining from condemning the practices of other cultures.

But of course the cultural relativists did not succeed in practice in abstaining from judging others. As a contemporary critic of *Patterns of Culture* observed of its author: "Try as she may to maintain the pose of relativism the test of consequences [or the use of value judgments] intrudes."[32] Indeed, as the American sociologist Philip Selznick has justly observed, Benedict's message was "not a justification for *every* form of life": she was ready to criticize the Kwakiutl pattern of rivalry as "enormously wasteful" and the Zuni as "incorrigibly mild." There may, as she claimed, be "equally valid" ways of life, but

> they all involve trade-offs, and some, such as the
> Dobuans, are hardly presented as admirable. Indeed,
> Benedict's work is full of evaluations. She had no
> qualms in describing Dobuans as "lawless and
> treacherous" or as "consumed with jealousy and
> suspicion and resentment." Nor did she hesitate to
> praise the Zuni for peaceful modes of interaction,
> benign forms of socialization, and freedom from a sense
> of sin. Most important, perhaps, is her statement that by
> raising consciousness about cultural determinism, "we
> may constrain ourselves to pass judgment upon the
> dominant traits of our own civilization."[33]

Boas and his followers were moral agents, active citizens who were politically engaged—engaged in combating ethnocentrism, intolerance, and racism at home and abroad. However, their doctrine became hard to defend in the face of Nazism. As Redfield remarked, "It was easy to look with equal benevolence upon all sorts of value systems so long as the values were those of unimportant little people remote from our own concerns. But the equal benevolence is harder to maintain when one is asked to anthropologize the Nazis."[34]

In the postwar context, cultural relativism seemed less and less relevant, not least because, as Margaret Mead put it, many non-Western peoples began "clamoring for the blessings of the modern world, machine technology, universal literacy, [and] medicine." Meanwhile, she added, anthropologists were "still trapped in a one-sided picture," regarding them as victims, not agents.[35] In 1947 anthropologists tried to persuade the United Nations Commission on Human Rights to adopt moral relativism. The executive board of the American Anthropological Association, led by Herskovits, submitted a statement proposing that the forthcoming UN Universal Declaration of Human Rights "be applicable to all human beings and not be a statement of rights conceived only in terms of the values prevalent in the countries of Western Europe and America." The declaration, they argued, should be "a statement of the rights of men to live in terms of their own traditions." Man is free, they confusingly declared, "only when he lives as his society defines freedom."[36] (What about traditions that do not value freedom?) The attempt failed, and a discourse on human rights that boldly assumed consensus across those traditions came to predominate across the world for several decades.

Nevertheless, the cultural relativists' ideas have had an impact that extends far beyond the confines of professional anthropology. They helped to unsettle unquestioned assumptions about the superiority of Western civilization and to encourage the suspicion that partisan interests—labeled "cultural or moral imperialism"—often lurk in ambush behind the universalistic language of human rights. Such universalism comes to be viewed as ethnocentric, centered on the West and North, and the defense of cultural particularity becomes a universal theme. The cultural relativists doubtless contributed to what Marshall Sahlins has called the remarkable "cultural self-consciousness among imperialism's erstwhile victims" that has "proliferated across the world."[37] In this way the practice of cultural imperialism has exported the very notion of culture. Cultural relativists reinforced twentieth-century doubts that our moral certainties are grounded in solid foundations, doubts that have inspired grave concern among religious leaders, not least the Pope. And their conceptions of *culture* and *enculturation* planted a series of questions for future research and reflection, questions that continue to confront and trouble us. To what extent are cultures, as they thought, bounded, internally consistent, and integrated (a question to which we will turn in Chapter 4)? Is there no distinction, as they also thought, between *morality* and *mores*, between what is moral and what is conventional? And how is that distinction to be understood? How does what they called "enculturation" work? How do we acquire our cultural beliefs and traits? When do we hold them to be "sacred" and beyond criticism? Is such criticism not an essential part of the moral life? When we make moral judgments, do we do so largely emotionally and unconsciously, only subsequently "propping them up," as Montaigne put it, with rational justifications? Was David Hume right to think that reason is "the slave of the passions," or was Kant right to think that our moral judgments flow from conscious, reasoned deliberation? And with respect to our moral intuitions, judgments, and behavior, what is

innate, what is learned, and what is the scope for rational reflection?

The Moral Psychologists

These are all live issues that have been increasingly
studied in recent years by psychologists, notably in the
growing field of moral psychology. Until the mid-1990s
it was widely assumed by psychologists that moral judgments and moral behavior are driven by conscious reasoning. The doyen of this "rationalist" tradition of moral
psychology was Lawrence Kohlberg, who was deeply
influenced by the ideas of the great Swiss psychologist
Jean Piaget, famous for his influential theory of cognitive
development and his theory of "genetic epistemology."
For Piaget, moral development in children proceeded
from "heteronomous," or self-centered, to "autonomous,"
or cooperative, stages of reasoning. Kohlberg elaborated
this into a theory of moral development according to
which there are three levels of reasoning—preconven-
tional, conventional, and postconventional—leading to
the highest stages of postconventional morality, which
consisted in a principled, democratic, individualist,
mutual acceptance of the rights and principles of justice. For Kohlberg, development culminates (though
not in everyone) in universal ethical principles and reciprocal role-taking, involving individual reasoning independently of authorities. In this picture moral
reasoning derives from the cognitive abilities people
have at successive stages of their development and from
the interaction between these and their social contexts.
From the standpoint of this theory, different societies
and cultures are viewed not as morally diverse, but as

either more or less conducive to what is assumed to be a "normal" development from heteronomous, conventional morals to the higher stages of mature, autonomous, universalizing, and individualist morality favoring democracy, justice, and rights.

From within this tradition Carol Gilligan criticized Kohlberg's theory for its focus on justice and rights to the exclusion of a supposedly less impersonal ethic focused on "care," interrelatedness, and empathy.[38] The first focuses on doing the right thing even if it requires personal cost or sacrificing the interest of those to whom one is close; the second, on putting the interests of those who are close to us above the interests of complete strangers. Gilligan claimed this alternative ethic to be distinctive of women, but this claim has not been accepted as proved by adequate and replicable evidence.

Eliot Turiel and his colleagues engaged in research that seemed to show that, rather than normally developing toward a fully autonomous way of moral reasoning, children from a very early age are able to distinguish between the domains of the moral and the conventional.[39] Children, they claimed, can distinguish between and react differently to moral norms (don't lie) and conventional norms (don't belch). In particular, they distinguish between rules prohibiting injury, theft, or promise-breaking, on the one hand, and rules prohibiting inappropriate dress, bad manners, or talking in class when not called on by the teacher, on the other. Moral transgressions, these psychologists claimed, are more serious, usually involve harming a victim or victims, are independent of the say-so of authorities, and involve rules that are general in scope and are justified by appeal to harm, justice, or rights. Conventional transgressions, by contrast, are less serious, and the rules are dependent on the dictates of particular authorities, local in scope, and not justified by reference to harm, justice, or rights. They concluded that their subjects, when questioned about transgressions of rules of both types, judged this distinction between domains as psychologically real and important. The idea was that these are seen as distinct conceptual domains to which different responses are appropriate because compliance is justified by different kinds of reasons. Furthermore, they claimed that their conclusions were supported by evidence covering a wide variety of subjects from toddlers to adults across different nationalities and religions.

Some critics adduced contrary evidence.[40] Other criticisms amount to two main claims.[41] The first is that people, both in other cultures and in ours, often respond to what look like moral harms and injustices by treating them as merely conventional violations, viewing them as merely local and justified by the dictates of authority. Consider, for instance, the acceptance of torture or corporal punishment or, indeed, the death penalty. How should we understand compliance, and indeed collaboration, with the committing of atrocities during wartime? And the second is that people, both in other cultures and in ours, often react to what look like harmless violations of conventions, where justice and rights are not at issue, with moral outrage and disgust, even horror. Desecrating the national flag, mixed bathing, masturbation, consensual incest, homosexual sex, polluting encounters, and in general, the breaking of taboos and rules of etiquette in many situations are all examples. But as we shall see in the next chapter, these criticisms misfire, since the theory of Turiel and his colleagues is that it is the moral/conventional *distinction,* not its *content,* that is cross-culturally valid and that from a very early age children are able to question adult authority and local prescriptions. This theory is entirely compatible with people viewing what we see as harmful actions as the best thing to do and with their judging what we see as harmless as morally unacceptable.

The field of moral psychology moved away from this "rationalist" focus on modes of moral reasoning in the mid-1990s to a more "Humean," intuitionist picture. In this view moral judgments result from unconscious, automatic processes, and moral reasoning amounts to post-hoc rationalization. Drawing on the work of neuroscientists and testing their hypotheses in brain-imaging experiments, these psychologists argue that moral judgments are largely driven by moral emotions such as gratitude, shame, embarrassment, contempt, and, perhaps most importantly, disgust. Moral reasoning, in this account, serves to justify our moral beliefs and actions, which are in fact caused by unconscious intuitive processes. In support of this claim, a central figure of this school, Jonathan Haidt, has identified what he calls "moral dumbfounding," where people exhibit strong moral convictions they find difficult to justify. An example is their perplexity in finding reasons for their widespread condemnation of the following story: a brother and sister intend to make love once and only once, decide to keep it secret, take maximum protective measures, and share a wonderful sensual experience.[42]

Haidt argues that in justifying our emotion-driven judgments, we seek to impress people we like and fortify our self-image. Two of his papers are entitled "Intuitive Ethics: How Innately Prepared Intuitions Generate Culturally Variable Virtues"[43] and "The Emotional Dog and Its Rational Tail: A Social Intuitionist Approach to Moral Judgment."[44] Switching his metaphorical animals, Haidt has expressed his overall view by suggesting that "our divided self is like a rider on the back of an elephant" and that "we give far too much importance to the rider—conscious thought." His basic thought is that if

> you listen closely to moral arguments, you can sometimes hear something surprising: that it is really the elephant holding the reins, guiding the rider. It is the elephant who decides what is good and bad, beautiful or ugly. Gut feelings, intuitions, and snap judgments happen constantly and automatically (as Malcolm Gladwell described in *Blink*), but only the rider can string sentences together and create arguments to give to other people. In moral arguments, the rider goes beyond being just an adviser to the elephant; he becomes a lawyer, fighting in the court of public opinion to persuade others of the elephant's point of view.[45]

But maybe it is possible to synthesize these contrasting Kantian/rationalist and Humean/intuitionist perspectives. Another researcher in this tradition, Joshua Greene, pictures moral thinking as combining emotional responses and rational constructions and reconstructions and as shaped by both biological and cultural forces. Several widely discussed moral dilemmas illustrate this suggestion.

Consider, first, the so-called trolley problem, invented by philosophers to elicit intuitions about permissible killing. Is it permissible for someone in a trolley hurtling toward five people walking on the track to flip the switch, thereby diverting it to a side track where it will kill only one person? (Call this the *bystander* case.) Now suppose that the only way to avert the death of the five is to push a large, heavy person from a footbridge into the path of the train? (Call this the *footbridge* case.) Most people regard the second action as impermissible but the first as permissible. Why? There are further refinements. Suppose that there is a loop in the track, which goes back to the main track, on which there is a person who will stop the train, and that a switch will divert the train to the loop. (Call this the *loop-track* case.) Or suppose that there is a heavy stone that will stop the train on that track, with a man standing in front of it, who will be killed. (Call this the *man-in-front* case.)

Consider, second, the so-called crying baby dilemma. You are hiding from enemy soldiers with fellow villagers in a basement during wartime. You cover your baby's mouth to stop the sound of her crying. If you remove your hand, the soldiers will hear and all of you will be killed. Is it permissible to smother your baby to death to save yourself and the villagers? People find this troubling and differ in their answers but can be convinced that killing the baby is permissible. Why?

Consider, third, a question raised by the philosopher

Peter Singer. Why do most of us believe we have a strict obligation to save a nearby drowning child but no comparable obligation to save faraway sick and starving children through charitable donations? Why, in general, do we care far more about identifiable victims than about statistical deaths? Greene's answer to all these questions is that we respond emotionally to what is "up close and personal" and that such responses can conflict with what we conclude when we reason impersonally.

Philosophers draw a distinction between *deontological* ethics, which is all about following rules and acknowledging rights and duties, and *consequentialist* ethics, where the point is to produce the best overall consequences. So consequentialists say that killing one person to save others may, in certain situations, be the right thing to do, whereas deontologists hold that there are moral "side-constraints"—prohibitions or "commandments"—that block us from maximizing the good of all: that the end cannot justify the means. This contrast is also apparent in the ways people think about and justify punishment. Consequentialists focus on gauging its beneficial effects, notably deterrence and the containment of dangerous people, whereas deontologists are driven by a focus on retribution, concerned to give wrongdoers what they deserve.

Greene's striking suggestion is that deontological judgments tend to be driven by emotional responses, and that deontological philosophy is largely an exercise in rationalization. So, for instance, we try to explain the difference between diverting the trolley with a switch and pushing the heavy person from the foot-

bridge by distinguishing between intended and foreseen consequences. Similarly, we argue that killing
the man in front of the stone is more permissible than
if there is no stone. We reason (but as Montaigne
might ask, how reasonably?) that intended harm is
worse than harm that is foreseen but not directly intended. Consequentialist thinking, on the other hand,
weighing costs against benefits, is more cognitive because more impersonal and more likely to involve
genuine moral reasoning. Perhaps these are "two different ways of moral thinking, that have been part of
the human repertoire for thousands of years" and perhaps, given that "personal violence is evolutionarily
ancient, predating our recently-evolved human capacities for complex abstract reasoning, it should come
as no surprise if we have innate responses to personal
violence that are powerful, if rather primitive. That is,
we might expect humans to have negative emotional
responses to certain basic forms of interpersonal violence, where these responses evolved as a means of
regulating the behavior of creatures who are capable
of intentionally harming one another, but whose survival depends on cooperation and individual res-
traint."[46]

These responses can, however, be overcome, and indeed "brain-imaging results suggest that 'cognitive'
psychological processes can compete with the aforementioned emotional processes, driving people to approve
of personally harmful moral violations, primarily when
there is a strong consequentialist rationale for doing so,
as in the *crying baby* case."[47]

Perhaps, in short, this is how we can resolve

Montaigne's apparent contradictions. Perhaps when we are in the "grip of custom," we are motivated by moral emotions that are indeed "natural," or innate, which developed because they helped individuals spread their genes: they sounded alarm bells, offering reliable, immediate responses to recurring situations. Perhaps we "prop up" these emotional responses by elaborating deontological rationalizations with talk of the Moral Law and "rights" and with categorical and inflexible moral rules. And perhaps we sometimes overcome or bypass their influence by means of more complex and impersonal reasoning.

Greene's is, of course, only one possible explanation of the trolley and other dilemmas. It relies on the assumption that people are naturally utilitarian and brings in emotions to explain their departures from utilitarian reasoning. It also relies on what many regard as highly questionable speculations about evolutionary psychological mechanisms in the distant and unknowable past. Perhaps a simpler and more comprehensive explanation of these dilemmas is one that assumes nonutilitarian intuitions about fairness (so that, for instance, the man on the footbridge has a greater right to remain unharmed, since he has put himself in less danger than the man walking on the tracks). And there is a more general worry that should be considered: that this methodology, typical of this school of moral psychology, by presenting subjects with such hypothetical moral dilemmas, thinly described and largely free of potentially relevant contextual information, loads the dice in favor of conceiving of morality in a particular way.

The Universality and Diversity of Norms

Montaigne noticed both the universality and the diversity of norms—rules specifying which actions are permitted, which required, and which forbidden, which encouraged and which discouraged. Norms govern a vast range of activities, from rules about the disposal of dead bodies to those governing economic exchange, the selection of mates, and the conduct of warfare. At a high level of abstraction we can say that certain activities are normatively regulated everywhere, such as killing, violence, and sexual relations and sharing, reciprocating, and helping. Most, if not all, societies have rules governing the fair, or just, distribution of benefits and burdens and the avoidance of harms. But of course, once one descends from this height of abstraction, as countless authors from Montaigne to Westermarck have noted, the greatest diversity appears at the level of the *content* of specific rules—concerning, for instance, when killing is justified, when sexual relations are permissible, and what counts as "fairness," "benefits and burdens," and "harms," and also concerning the scope of the norms' application. Some societies include animals along with humans, others only humans, others only a subset of humans; and there is, of course, further variation in how these are ranked in respect of the importance accorded them. So, for example, norms against violence may exclude women or children or animals or marginalized subgroups or castes. In general, at this more specific level, norms cluster into patterns that differ from one another that we can call "cultures"—across which there is considerable diversity concerning what is permissible, what is obligatory, what is forbidden, what is encouraged and discouraged, and concerning who and what is worthy of concern.

Across all cultures humans seem to show the same automatic emotional responses to social interactions (indicated by facial expressions). Most cultures are alike in offering systems of justification for moral decisions that appeal to supernatural intentional agents, such as gods, spirits, and ancestors. These differ according to their different religious systems but seem in all cases to help resolve moral dilemmas and justify hard moral decisions. Most people (other than those with psychological deficits) reliably internalize the norms of their culture and do so at an early age. They are motivated to comply with them and to punish those who violate them. Very young children display what we may call moral capacities. They can reason about the rules and their violation and can distinguish between rule-governed and accidental regularities and between intentional and accidental violations, and they manifest punitive attitudes to norm violators. And from an even earlier age they show empathy and helping and comforting behavior. In short, while still very young, they are already primed to see themselves and others as moral agents intentionally performing actions whose different consequences they can begin to assess.

Furthermore, as Susan Dwyer summarizes the evidence,

> All (normal) humans develop into moral agents, that is, into creatures with (at least) the following moral capacities: the ability to make judgments about the moral permissibility, moral impermissibility, and moral

obligatoriness of actions in actual and hypothetical, novel and familiar cases; the ability to register morality's special authority (i.e. the fact that moral imperatives are nonhypothetically binding and sometimes contrary to self-interest); the ability to make attributions of moral responsibility for actions (as distinct from attributions of mere causal responsibility); and the ability to recognize the force of excuses.[48]

Moreover, there is a growing body of evidence from so-called experimental economics that reinforces and deepens this picture. By getting people across different cultures to play various ingeniously constructed "games," researchers have elicited evidence that people are very widely motivated to cooperate and comply with norms of reciprocity and fairness, norms that stabilize cooperation between individuals and within larger groups. These norms are followed for their own sake and not as a means to other ends. For instance, in the so-called ultimatum game, one player is given a sum of money, say ten dollars, and instructed to share it with a second player, on the understanding by both that, if the second player rejects what is offered, neither receives anything. It turns out that in most cases, and across cultures, people reject offers that are seen as unfairly low. There is a general expectation that 50-50 is fair, but this is not universal; for instance, there appears to be a greater readiness for exploitation in rural as opposed to urban cultures.[49]

This and similar evidence can be taken (with varying degrees of skepticism about what they are actually evidence of) to controvert the widespread assumption that people conform to the model of instrumentally rational *homo economicus,* invariably maximizing their individual self-interest. Interestingly, it also seems to confirm Kluckholm's suggestion that people are widely (though of course not invariably) motivated to punish the violation of such norms, and in proportion to the perceived seriousness of the violation; they do this even at substantial cost to themselves and even where their interests are not involved. Other researchers have confirmed that norm violations typically elicit punitive emotions like disgust, anger, and outrage and the behavior that expresses them, such as criticism, condemnation, avoidance, and exclusion, even the infliction of physical harm, and, not least, ostracism and gossip, which some suggest could well be cultural universals.

So we have a substantial and growing body of evidence that individuals universally comply with norms and exhibit moral capacities from a very early age but do so in divergent ways, obeying different norms and subscribing to different moral codes (which already appear in children between the ages of seven and nine). Humans share moral capacities but disagree over which actions are morally permissible, obligatory, and forbidden, encouraged or discouraged, and over who and what falls within the scope of moral concern. How are we best to explain this combination of moral unity and moral diversity?

The Linguistic Analogy

What we need to explain is that people universally acquire, at a very early age, the norms of their respective and divergent cultures, in ways that far exceed what they can have learned. This suggests that we need to postulate an innate psychological mechanism that enables human beings to see the world in moral terms, but to do so in ways that enable them to respond to different moral environments. Just as all children acquire knowledge of their language from a finite and fragmentary sample of its use and can thereafter understand and produce novel sentences they have never encountered before, so children's aforementioned moral capacities considerably exceed what they can have learned from observation of the varied and often highly confusing responses and instructions of parents or other caretakers.

This parallel has suggested to some that there may be an analogy between language and morality. According to Noam Chomsky's theory of generative linguistics, humans possess an innate linguistic competence that is universal in the species, consisting in principles and parameters, of which we are not conscious, that determine which are the humanly possible languages we can learn and speak. Languages are deeply structured in different ways to which the parameters correspond: they are like switches that when switched on render a language learnable. Each human language instantiates a particular setting of the parameters. Perhaps, several theorists have suggested, we have a "universal moral grammar" that similarly determines a range of humanly possible moralities. As Marc Hauser puts it, "Like language, the specifically expressed and culturally variable moral systems are learned in the sense that the detailed contents of particular social norms are acquired by exposure to the local culture; the abstract principles and parameters are innate."[50] And as Susan Dwyer writes, this model

> appears to have the attractive feature of suggesting an account of moral diversity, in much the same way that the principles and parameters theory in linguistics has actually provided an account of linguistic diversity. Universal moral grammar provides the cognitive resources that make possible the acquisition of moral capacities. Since the latter are acquired in particular moral environments, the developing moral agent will come to exercise them in ways that reflect those environments, and so will come to be able to negotiate moral space in ways that are sensitive to local conditions.[51]

If the linguistic analogy holds, then the principles of "universal moral grammar" operate below the level of consciousness, and so, in Hauser's words, "people tend to make moral judgments without being aware of the underlying principles," and so "for a wide range of moral dilemmas we deliver rapid judgments in the absence of coherent justifications."[52] This would offer one explanation of the findings, mentioned above, that moral judgments can be emotion-driven and that explicit reasoning serves to "prop them up" by adducing socially acceptable justifications.

But the linguistic analogy has shortcomings. For one thing, conflicting linguistic intuitions are not like conflicting moral intuitions. The former get resolved pragmatically and do not interfere with our linguistic practice, whereas the latter typically give rise to moral dilemmas. Secondly, moral maturity is unlike linguistic facility: once we have acquired a language, we use it spontaneously and without doubts and hesitations, whereas for many people the moral life is riddled with these, and serious moral thinking precisely consists in wrestling with them. Thirdly, ordinary language users do not have access to the underlying principles governing their linguistic competence, and their performance as language users is unaffected if linguistic experts enable them to acquire it. But as Hauser observes, "it is possible that even without any access to the underlying principles, or with only limited access, the nature of our moral judgments shifts once we *become* aware of these principles. . . . [T]he moral faculty may guard its principles but once its guard has been penetrated, we may use these principles to guide how we consciously reason about morally permissible actions."[53]

So on this account it would appear that we can, after all, engage in rational deliberation and reflection on our moral principles and that, as I have suggested, when we do this we can adjudicate between conflicting intuitions and can override them. But according to generative linguistics, our universal grammar delivers *one or another* language, depending on which set of parameters is "switched on." We end up speaking one language, or indeed several, and there is no Esperanto-like location from which we can reach what is rationally required as the *right* way to speak. In short, taking the linguistic analogy seriously would drive us straight to moral relativism, for we could not arrive at the judgment that there is a right way to act. We would have to believe that our human moral competence can only issue in judgments about what is right relatively to one morality or another.[54]

One obvious response to the relativist is to adopt the distinction made in the previous chapter between the internal and the external senses of morality. From the internal, participant's perspective, the moral life consists, of course, in conscious reasoning, which, moreover, can take many different forms, from abstract theorizing to the telling of parables. Clearly, when facing our doubts and hesitations, confronting moral dilemmas, and arriving at moral judgments, we weigh competing considerations (and sometimes decide that they cannot be weighed), we figure out which are relevant and which have priority. We appeal to principles, we draw on relevant experiences, examples, and stories. We think ourselves into other people's shoes, even try to get inside their skins. When faced with a moral issue or problem or dilemma, in other words, we use our imagination and our intellect to try hard to arrive at *the right answer.*

Moral relativists will very likely concede that this is indeed the way things look from the inside but will go on to suggest that our judgments are, as Westermarck thought, formulated in ways calculated to give moral values an objectivity they do not possess. And they may well add that what looks, from the inside, like reasoned deliberation and reflection aiming at the right answer exhibits, from the outside, different and conflicting styles of reasoning.

We have been assuming until now that this picture of the fact of moral *diversity,* which, as I suggested, motivates the moral relativist, is an accurate, or at least plausible, picture. But is it? That is the question to which the next chapter is addressed.

3

THE DIVERSITY OF MORALS

> To determine the extent and the nature of diversity in
> moral judgments is a matter which presents great
> difficulties.   MORRIS GINSBERG[1]

The picture is of moral norms clustering into distinct moralities, which are diverse because they issue alternative directives for action. Norms, as we said, answer the question Which actions are required, prohibited, permitted, discouraged, and encouraged? The idea of diversity suggests that, from within different moral codes, different answers emerge. There are, then, two questions that we must address. First, what distinguishes *moral* from other norms? And second, how different must these answers be if we are to speak of *diversity*?

The Moral Domain (1)

I have already suggested that moral norms cover matters of importance in people's lives. They are directed at promoting good and avoiding evil, at encouraging virtue and discouraging vice, at avoiding harm to others and promoting their well-being or welfare. They are concerned with the interests of others or the common interest rather than just with the individual's self-interest, and they are distinct from the rules and principles of etiquette, law, and religion—though the conduct they enjoin may overlap with what these enjoin. This last point implies that some rules of etiquette (governing, say, hospitality or filial respect), legal rules (prohibiting, say theft and violence), and religious rules (prescribing, say, conduct at sacred rituals) can be invested with moral significance, while others (such as forms of greeting, traffic laws, or minor ritual rules) may not.

An alternative approach is to suggest ways in which people register the differences between what is moral and what is not. Scanlon proposes that they accord moral requirements extreme importance, that they feel guilt or self-reproach when they violate them, and that victims of such violations feel resentment and indignation, while compliance with moral requirements is accepted by others.[2]

Jon Elster, the Norwegian social theorist, distinguishes between moral, quasi-moral, social, and legal norms, while recognizing that the dividing lines are fluid. Moral and quasi-moral norms can shape behavior even when the agent believes herself unobserved. Moral norms are unconditional (such as helping others in distress, equal sharing, and "everyday Kantianism"—doing what would be best if everyone did the same). Quasi-moral norms are conditional (such as the norm of reciprocity—help those who help you and harm those who harm you; and the norm of conditional cooperation—cooperate if others do, but not otherwise). Social norms are triggered when others can observe what one is doing, and involve shame. Legal norms are enforced by specialized agents who typically impose direct punishment.[3]

Some, such as Marc Hauser, have suggested that the domain of the moral is registered by emotion and a sense of seriousness. So Hauser writes that a "central difference between social conventions and moral rules is the seriousness of an infraction. When someone violates a moral rule, it feels more serious; transgressions in the conventional domain tend to be associated with a relatively cool or neutral emotional response—eating with elbows on the dinner table is poor etiquette in some cultures, but certainly not an event that triggers passionate outrage."[4] But this is quite unconvincing if intended as a criterion for distinguishing moral from conventional norms, for people can often exhibit violent emotions at the flouting of conventions. For instance, Elster recounts the story of a young officer in pre-Revolutionary France, wealthy but not noble, who, having tried to gate-crash a party at Versailles, was driven to suicide by the ridicule with which he was greeted.[5] Conversely, people can often be coolly rational in their moral judgments. As Dwyer has observed, some parents "get just as hot under the collar about conventional transgressions as they do about moral transgressions," and "even adults have difficulty distinguishing between strong emotional reactions," which is why it is "hardly likely that very young children are any better at making fine-grained discriminations between the emotion-laden responses of their caretakers."[6]

The question of what distinguishes moral from conventional norms is therefore far from straightforward—not least because most people in most contexts for most of the time adhere to conventional morals and may well, as Montaigne suggested, have good reasons and be well advised to do so. Let us then, for the time being, accept the broad and loose way of distinguishing what is moral by combining the various suggestions above, and next ask in what moral diversity consists. When following different moral norms results in different actions, what degree and kind of difference will license talk of moral diversity?

The Right Description

There appears to be a continuum here stretching from the weakest to the strongest instances. At the weakest end, two actions can be said to be different merely because they are different ways of accomplishing the same acceptable end. Examples are alternative forms of marriage or (to recall Herodotus) disposing of the dead. Here you could speak of moral diversity meaning merely that two moral codes govern variants of the same practice. At the strongest end are cases where the actions in question exclude one another, so that what one moral code prohibits the other allows, encourages, or even requires: for example, female circumcision or the killing of aged parents. Less strong, but still at the strong end of the continuum, are cases where the behavior resulting from following one code's norms contrasts with that resulting from following another's. Examples of such contrasts are actions manifesting more patriarchal versus more egalitarian relations between men and women or between parents and children. Moral relativists, clearly, are interested in the stronger end of this continuum, where the norms of what are seen as distinct moralities issue conflicting or, at the extreme, incompatible directives for action: that is, require different actions, not different ways of performing the same action. They are interested in cases, such as those indicated above, where, as Cook succinctly puts it, "a mode of conduct which among one people is condemned as wrong is among other people viewed with indifference or enjoined as a duty."[7]

But how are we to decide which cases to place at the weak and which at the strong end of this weak-strong continuum? How are we to decide when two actions are merely variant ways of *doing the same acceptable thing* rather than conflicting or incompatible alternatives? Consider the examples cited above. Modern Westerners see arranged marriages as imposed and sometimes coercive, whereas for traditionalists from the Asian subcontinent to marry in the Western way is to be footloose and irresponsible. Or are the two forms perhaps just alternative dating services? As for the disposal of corpses, Herodotus informs us that the Greeks and Callatiae each regarded the other's practice not just as an alternative method or means but as an abomination.

Conversely, the debate that has raged over female circumcision has in part been about how to characterize the practice. In one view it should be called "female genital mutilation" on the ground that the usual ways of performing it are painful, preclude sexual pleasure, cause numerous immediate and long-term health complications, especially at childbirth, and often result in psychological disturbances. To many who have studied it or campaigned against it, it is a classic case of violation of the human right to bodily integrity. However, the practice, which is often accompanied by ceremonies to honor and welcome the girls into their communities, is locally held to promote "normal" gender identity, improve their bodies aesthetically, maintain cleanliness and health, preserve virginity and family honor, prevent immorality, and further marriage goals, including greater sexual pleasure for men. So the anthropologist Richard Shweder, in the name of "engaging cultural differences," denounces liberals and feminists for their misunderstanding and suggests calling the practice "female genital modification."[8] And what are we to say of Redfield's Eskimos walling up their aged parents? Are they engaged in homicide or are these really assisted suicides?

The question is: how are we to decide what an action or practice is *really*? Among the many plausible descriptions of it, which is the correct one? Is this question decidable? Does it have an answer? We want to know what is going on, what the actors are up to. At the very least we want to know what the meaning of the action or practice is in its context for the actors involved. But in seeking to know at least this, major obstacles lie in wait for us.

First, there are, of course, several, sometimes many actors involved, so the question is: meaning for whom? Consider, for example, the case of *suttee*, or widow-burning, in India. How do widows view this religiously sanctioned ritual? On September 4, 1987, Roop Kanwar, a beautiful eighteen-year-old college-educated Rajput woman, received national press coverage in India when she immolated herself before a large and supportive crowd, her dead husband resting in her lap. The anthropologist Richard Shweder, who tells this story, imagines her "conception of things," suggesting that "it is conceivable that Roop Kanwar herself understood and experienced her immolation as an astonishing moment when her body and its senses, profane things, became fully sacred, and hence invulnerable to pain, through an act of sacrifice by a goddess seeking eternal union with her god-man."[9] On the other hand, as Shweder concedes, critics of the practice of suttee argued that either "Roop Kanwar must have been forced to the funeral pyre, where she must have been agitated and wanted to flee; or . . . [she] must have been drugged or hysterical or crazy."[10]

Or take the case of Franca Viola, a young Sicilian woman, whose story is cited by Cook, quoting an Associated Press dispatch from Alcamo, Sicily. Franca "broke a thousand years of Sicilian tradition" by refusing "to wed the rich man's son who kidnapped and raped her. Since the Middle Ages, kidnap and rape have been the sure road to the altar for a rejected Sicilian suitor. If the girl didn't say yes after that, she was dishonored and no-one else would marry her." Franca then took her rich suitor to court, charging him with rape, and in consequence she and her family "were threatened with vengeance for her violation of the ancient code."[11] She subsequently married another man, who carried a gun on their wedding day for protection.

Or consider, finally, the case, cited by Redfield, of the Pawnee "Knife Chief" and his son, who repeatedly tried, and failed, to end the custom of human sacrifice in which young girls from other tribes were killed, regarding it as "an unnecessary and cruel exhibition of power, exercised upon unfortunate and defenseless individuals whom they were bound to protect."[12]

The first two examples illustrate the general truth that the morality prevalent in a culture will normally implement the self-serving interests of the powerful (which their victims may appear, less or more completely, to endorse); while the third shows that the power of the chief and his son is structurally embedded, resisting innovative efforts by individuals, however powerful.

The second obstacle to deciding what an action or practice is "really" is the very general one of correctly identifying the conduct in question. Assuming there to be a correct description of the alien action or practice in question, how is it to be attained? Consider the case of usury—the practice of lending money for interest—condemned as immoral, even sinful, in medieval times but becoming respectable with the rise of commerce and industrial investments. The Gestalt psychologist Karl Duncker cited this in a most interesting article, asking: "do we in both cases deal with the same act?" For in the earlier period "loans were employed predominantly for consumption, whereas in capitalism loans are employed mainly as capital for profitable production. That makes all the difference. Where the borrower borrows in order to gain, it is only fair to make the lender a partner in the undertaking by paying him some "share in the profit." Interest no longer means an exploitation of necessities or passions. It has changed its typical 'meaning.'"[13]

Or consider the observation of Kenneth Dover, in his classic study of popular morality in ancient Greece, that given the structure of Greek society, "it would be surprising if identical moral judgments were passed on the same dishonest, selfish or aggressive act irrespective of whether it was committed against a relative or a stranger, a man or a woman, a citizen or a foreigner, a freeborn man or a slave." For the Greeks "might not have agreed with us in calling two acts 'the same'; they would have been inclined to feel that our description stopped short of the complete act if it did not take into account the limits of the victim's expectations and the extent to which the act could affect his status in the eyes of others."[14]

The Projection Error and the Projection Problem
Typically this problem of finding the right description of acts takes the form, already alluded to, of avoiding what Cook calls "the projection error." (Evans-Pritchard called it the "If I were a horse fallacy."[15]) This occurs when we misunderstand the beliefs and motives of another people because we are "prone to project onto them assumptions derived from our own culture." The error often consists in mistakenly believing that "the conduct which is condemned in our culture is the *same* conduct that is condoned in some other."[16] Cook cites several telling instances of anthropologists' recognition of this error at work. One observes an Eskimo community forcing a young orphan boy to forage for food among voracious battling dogs and assumes them to be callously indifferent to his plight, but then learns that their greatest hunters are orphans and the boy was being "hardened for a better life."[17] Raymond Firth reports that in his study of the Tikopia he first "came to the conclusion that there was no such thing as friendship or kindness for its own sake among these people," because they were always demanding and never offering things, but came to realize that for them "the most

obvious foundation of friendship was material reciprocity" and that their constant demands were "overtures
and a testing of the waters of friendship."[18] And Malinowski recalls that his first impression of the Trobri-
and islanders was that their chiefs were tyrannical and
greedy, exacting sexual, economic, and personal advantages, including enormous tribute, especially in food.
But he then reflects that fuller knowledge "convinced
me that I had been in error," for the "enormous tribute,
which the chief collects in food he does not, in fact he
could not, consume himself. He employs it in ceremo-
nial redistributions, in financing war, enterprise and
tribal festivity." The organizing power and accumulated
resources of the chief provide the commoners with what
makes "life worth living for them."[19]

Detecting the projection error is not, however, always
straightforward. Cook also claims that Ruth Benedict
committed it in her famous paper "Anthropology and
the Abnormal," in which she claimed that "normality, . . .
within a very wide range, is culturally defined."[20] For
instance, she claimed that a "[b]ehavior honored upon
the Northwest coast is one which is recognized as abnormal in our civilization."[21] The Kwakiutl were, by our
standards, megalomaniacs since, during their potlatches, "there was an uncensored self-glorification and
ridicule of the opponent that it is hard to equal in other
cultures outside of the monologues of the abnormal."[22]
But, writes Cook, megalomaniacs are "acting out some
pathological fantasy of their own," whereas the Kwakiutl "have been taught since childhood to participate
in potlatches, and what they say on those occasions is
largely a matter of ritual." Benedict similarly claims that

the Kwakiutl see insults everywhere, even in accidental events, and this by our standards calls for a diagnosis of paranoia. But, writes Cook, their seeing accidents as insults is "not the outcome of some irrational fear or suppressed hostility" but a pattern learned from the elders. In short, Benedict makes the mistake of "equating actions in one culture with those in another because of their superficial resemblance."[23]

But Cook underestimates the subtlety of Benedict's argument. It is true that it is here that she states her unfortunate slogan that "morality differs in every society and is a convenient term for socially approved habits."[24] But she also writes, with respect to psychiatry, that "the very eyes with which we see the problem are conditioned by long traditional habits of our own society,"[25] and she warns that the information we possess about the behavior of the unstable in other cultures "does not correspond to data from our own society."[26] Given these caveats, her focus is rather on the ways in which different cultural environments value and honor or discourage and stifle a range of personalities, interior states, and conduct: culture, she writes, "may value and make available even highly unstable human types."[27] Various cultures may encourage "extreme psychic manifestations" like trance and epilepsy and value and accord them prestige. An adult shaped to the drives and standards of other cultures, "if he were transported into our civilization, would fall into our categories of abnormality. He would be faced with the psychic dilemmas of the socially unavailable. In his own culture, however, he is the pillar of society, the end result of socially inculcated mores, and the problem of personal instability in his case simply does not arise."[28] Benedict's central idea is that from all we know of the evidence of contrasting cultures,

> it seems clear that differences of temperament occur in every society. The matter has never been made the subject of investigation, but from the available material it would appear that these temperament types are very likely of universal recurrence. That is, there is an ascertainable range of human behavior that is found wherever a sufficiently large series of individuals is observed. The vast majority of individuals in any group are shaped to the fashion of that culture. In other words, most individuals are plastic to the moulding force of the society into which they are born. . . . In a society that institutionalizes homosexuality, they will be homosexual.[29]

So it is clear that what Benedict is comparing here is not conduct erroneously projected, but rather alternative settings that either encourage or discourage a range of personality types and forms of conduct to emerge and be valued.

Nevertheless, one can see how easy it is to commit the projection error and how short a step it is from doing so to embracing moral relativism. Having misidentified a given mode of conduct as the same conduct that in our culture we would judge negatively, you simply withdraw the judgment and say that they practice what we wrongly condemn, claiming, following Benedict's slogan, that "morality differs in every society and is a convenient term for socially approved habits." Cook, indeed, advances the intriguing and plausible suggestion that Franz Boas, universally regarded as the father of cultural relativism, was in fact not a relativist at all and that his central message was, rather, an argument against faulty cultural comparisons due to "overlooking, on account of general resemblance, significant dissimilarities"[30]—that his idea, in short, was that in order to understand the thoughts of a people, "the whole analysis . . . must be based on their concepts, not ours."[31] Boas was in fact concerned to combat the prevalent denigration of other cultures and show it to be unwarranted. In Cook's interpretation, he took this position not because he was a relativist but because of his insight into the projection error. We condemned other cultures because we mistakenly believed their practices to be analogous to practices that in our own culture were viewed as unfair, cruel, or vicious. And it is indeed true that Boas wrote that "the study of human cultures should not lead to a relativistic attitude toward ethical standards."[32]

But this leads us to a further major obstacle in our attempt to decipher the meaning of conduct in other cultural settings. This obstacle is really a radicalization or deepening of the previous one. To speak, as Cook does, of the projection *error* is to assume that there is an ascertainable truth of the matter about which one is in error, just as Boas assumes that, to avoid it, we can gain access to "their concepts." But how do we gain such access other than by rendering the unfamiliar familiar through analogy—by finding in our own culture appropriate analogies for practices in alien cultural settings? How, in any given case, do we determine which analogy is appropriate? Perhaps, at least sometimes, there is no single definitively right or correct answer to be found. At the very least, a measure of skepticism is appropriate here as to whether we have found it.

Consider the example of a gruesome practice that used to exist among the Dinka of the Southern Sudan, namely, the custom of burying alive certain very respected and religious leaders. These leaders, called the spearmasters, would each be placed in a specially dug hole. Each would then have cattle dung heaped upon him until he suffocated to death.[33] Apparently, the Dinka believed that the spearmasters were repositories of the vital force of the tribe and its cattle and that this ritual enabled that force to be passed on to allow the tribe to flourish; moreover, the spearmasters, at the end of their natural lives, announced that their time to die had come. So is John Kekes right to suggest that "[l]ive burial for them is like donating blood or a kidney is for us. . . . It is true that both blood or kidney donors and spearmasters suffer various degrees of injury, but it is in a good cause, and both the altruistic victims and beneficiaries see it as such"?[34] Is the killing of the Dinka leaders, like that of aged parents among Eskimos, to be described as "assisted suicide"? Is the young orphan boy being given leadership training like a Boy Scout? Are arranged marriages like dating services? Obviously, these analogies are, like all analogies, imperfect, and it is a matter of contestable judgment how well an analogy may apply in any given case. If finding such analogies is our means of access to the concepts of others, perhaps we must conclude that there is a certain ethnocentrism or what we might call 'methodological narcissism'" that is inescapable when we are faced with judgments and practices that raise the issue of moral diversity.

And there is a further difficulty to consider. In the Boas-Cook view, in seeking the right description of the conduct of others, we should avoid projecting our assumptions and instead base our analysis on their concepts. But is this always *appropriate*? I return here to the question, adumbrated earlier, of whether we merely want to know the meaning of the conduct in its context for the actors involved. Do we not want to insist that Franca Viola's rich suitor *raped* her, and do we not want to do so, whether or not he and the local community so described his action? Indeed, even if, among all the women who have been treated as she was, there may have been many who would not have so described it, does that mean that we should not do so? And what about the immolation of Roop Kanwar? Suppose that her conception of things was as Shweder imagines. Would this constitute the last word from *our* point of view as observers and would-be explainers? The condition of widows in India is traditionally highly oppressive and can be desperately so. As Martha Nussbaum has observed, "*sati* [suttee] would always be suspect, even when practiced entirely within a religious tradition, because its voluntariness is generally suspect."[35] In general, to be adequate from our standpoint, any description of actions and practices must be thick enough (that is: incorporate enough contextual information) to capture the impact of power relations of domination or oppression. This is no less true where there is reason to think that victims consent out of powerlessness.

These are formidable obstacles, but let us assume

that they are not insuperable. Let us suppose that we have overcome them: that we are satisfied that we are confronting a case where the norms of one culture or people condemn conduct as wrong that is elsewhere viewed with indifference or enjoined as a duty. The next question is: are we confronting a genuine case of moral *diversity*?

Genuine Moral Diversity?

(1) DIRE NECESSITY

We might not be, for either of two reasons. The first is that the conduct in question might be best explained as a response to dire necessity. Consider the horrifying lives of the members of the Ik tribe of northeastern Uganda, memorably described by the anthropologist Colin Turnbull in his controversial book *The Mountain People*.[36] The Ik had been driven from their traditional hunting grounds in order to create a national park and, according to Turnbull, were forced to become farmers, with no knowledge of farming, in a land without rain. As a result they were starving, family life had disintegrated, children stole food from the old, parents allowed their children to starve to death, and the aged and the ill were left to die. "Acute hunger and the physical hardship of the food quest," writes Turnbull, "obviously weakened the sexual appetites of the Ik, and in so doing, it deprived them of a major drive toward sociality and confirmed them in their solitariness."[37] He describes them as living "without love"[38] and as lacking "any sense of moral responsibility toward each other" and "any sense of belonging to, needing or wanting each other."[39] He observes that the misfortune of others "was their greatest joy, and I wondered whether in their minds it lessened the probability of misfortune visiting them or increased it. But personal misfortune was really beyond the realm of probability, it was a certainty. So cruelty was with them, in their humor, in their interpersonal relations, in their thoughts and reflections. Yet so utter was their isolation, as individuals, that I do not think they thought of their cruelty as affecting others."[40] Turnbull reflects that the Ik had "learned to do without coercion, either spiritual or physical" and that it seemed that they had "come to a recognition of what they accept as man's basic selfishness, of his natural determination to survive as an individual before all else."[41] The anthropologist Rodney Needham once described Turnbull's book to me as an instance of concentration camp literature, and indeed Turnbull himself comments that it "was rare for man to shed so much of his 'humanity'" as among the Ik, "though it happened, at Treblinka and elsewhere."[42]

This example is like that of the Inuit's killing of infants and the unproductive elderly: as Neil Levy suggests, the Inuit did this, not because they "did not care for the children or aged parents, nor because they did not respect human life, but because they could only ensure the survival of some by killing others."[43] Indeed, Levy continues, we can similarly explain why girls suffered disproportionately, for among the Inuit the males did the hunting, which was dangerous, with a high casualty rate, and so "a higher proportion of male children needed to be reared, to maintain approximately equal sex ratios among the adults."[44] Perhaps, as Turnbull suggests, among the Ik the harsh conditions of life had a deeper impact in shaping their attitudes and feelings, but in neither case are we licensed to conclude that their indifference to or approval of actions we condemn betokens an alternative morality. What they suggest, rather, is that when conditions become dire enough, the scope for moral judgment and behavior can be eclipsed by the struggle to survive in a war of all against all.

(2) FACTUAL AND MORAL DISAGREEMENTS

But there is a second reason why we may not wish to conclude that conflicting moral norms, in the sense indicated, signify genuine moral diversity. One culture or people or group may condemn what another views with indifference or enjoins as a duty, but the explanation for this may lie in their embracing alternative factual beliefs while sharing a common moral code. For there to be moral diversity there must be what the philosopher Richard Brandt calls "fundamental moral disagreement," which exists "only if ethical appraisals or valuations are incompatible, even where there is mutual agreement between the relevant parties concerning the nature of the act that is being appraised."[45] To take Brandt's simplified example, suppose that one group approves of children executing their parents at a certain age or state of feebleness, while another group strongly disapproves of this. It may be that "in the first group the act is thought necessary for the welfare of the parent in the afterlife, whereas in the second group it is not thought to be." The disagreement "might well be removed by agreement about the facts, and indeed both parties might subscribe to the principle 'It is right for a child to treat a parent in whatever way is required for the parent's long-term welfare.' The disagreement might be simply about the implications of this common principle, in the light of differing conceptions of the facts."[46]

Now, the virtue of this last example, as of all philosophers' examples, is that, being thinly, or abstractly, described and simple, it enables us to focus in an analytical way on conceptual distinctions that clarify the issue under discussion. In this case, it points us to the distinction between a shared moral principle and divergent factual beliefs. On the other hand, such simplifications can be misleading when we try to think about real-world cases. So, considering this example, is it really so obvious that a disagreement that hinges on the afterlife would be regarded by both parties to the disagreement as a *factual* one? Might not those who deny that there can be welfare after death claim that the very idea of the afterlife is a *fiction*—and indeed a fiction part of whose point is to bolster a certain moral outlook? In that case there would be no truth of the matter—no truth conditions that could determine whether belief in what happens in the afterlife is true or false (so that it is neither true nor false). And might they not further hold that such beliefs are, in any case, not real beliefs but rather half-formed quasi-beliefs that are inherently incoherent (what does it *mean* to live after life, and what could *welfare* mean after death, and so on)?

But if philosophers' examples are oversimplified, the ethnographic accounts of anthropologists are insufficiently analytical. One problem is what Moody-Adams calls the "artificiality of the anthropologist's 'ethnographic present,'" which "fails to suggest the inherent potential for ongoing evolution of complex moral practices."[47] Furthermore, in most anthropological works, as the French anthropologist and cognitive scientist Dan Sperber has remarked, the reader "is directly presented with an elaborate interpretation in the form of a consolidated, complex, and coherent discourse (with just occasional translations of native statements and descriptions of anecdotes by way of illustration). Such interpretations are related to actual data in poorly understood, unsystematic and generally unspecified ways."[48]

Ethnographic accounts, in short, are thick (that is, fully contextualized) descriptions of others' beliefs and practices, which do not, however, license us to infer how far any given disagreement between their norms and ours derives from a fundamental moral disagreement rather than a factual one. Brandt rightly comments that the material assembled, for instance, by Westermarck simply shows that various peoples approve of or condemn lying, suicide, industry, cleanliness, adultery, homosexuality, cannibalism, and so on. But this, of course, is not enough, for we need to know how those various peoples *conceive* of these things: "Do they eat human flesh because they like its taste, or do they kill slaves merely for the sake of a feast? Or do they eat flesh because they think it is necessary for tribal fertility, or because they think they will then participate in the manliness of the person eaten? Perhaps those who condemn cannibalism would not do so if they thought that eating the flesh of an enemy is necessary for the survival of the group."[49]

Brandt observed that "no anthropologist has offered what we should regard as really an adequate account of a single case, clearly showing that there is ultimate disagreement in ethical principle,"[50] and so he himself undertook research into the moral life of the Hopi of the American Southwest. His resulting study, *Hopi Ethics,* tentatively explores this problem by asking whether, across a range of morally relevant issues, one can find "behavior toward which there is a basic difference of attitude between Hopi and white Americans [*sic*]—a difference of attitude along with identity of factual beliefs."[51] He finds one example that seems to him clearer than others: cruelty to animals. Hopi children often catch birds and play with them by tying their legs, breaking them, and then pulling their wings off. Brandt comments that "Hopi disapproval of cruelty to animals seems weaker than that of a large segment of white American opinion. Moreover, where Hopi beliefs about animals differ from white American beliefs, they are of a kind that one would have expected to cause more concern about the welfare of animals, not less. For Hopi do not regard animals as unconscious or insensitive; they rather regard them as closer to the human species than does the average white man [*sic*]."[52]

We shall return to this example, which is interesting for a number of reasons. For one thing, it is, as Brandt himself recognized, open to various alternative interpretations, for "one may wonder if Hopi have the suffering of animals as clearly and vividly in mind as does the average white American who objects to maltreatment of animals. Or it might be argued that Hopi do not really have an equally strong sentiment for human beings, for, if they did, they would also be more interested in the suffering of animals than they are."[53] Secondly, it is interesting because the treatment of animals only became a matter of moral concern in the late eighteenth century; before then the difference of attitude between "us" and "them" would have seemed much less clear.[54] Which suggests, thirdly, that the distinction between what is moral and what is conventional is complex, contingent, and historically shifting.

Three Examples

Brandt's example is interesting for a further reason. It suggests that fundamental moral disagreements that do not derive from factual ones may often be found where there are divergent assumptions about the *scope* of moral concern. If so, we can perhaps view the life story of the Spanish priest Bartolomé de Las Casas as revealing a case of genuine moral diversity—in this case experienced by the same individual. Columbus and the early Spanish explorers treated the American natives with extreme brutality. According to a 1530 judicial report to Charles V, they treated them "as dogs." Las Casas witnessed this treatment, reporting that the Spaniards "made bets as to who would slit a man in two, or cut off his head at one blow; or they opened up his bowels. They tore the babies from their mother's breast by their feet, and dashed their heads against the rocks. . . ."[55] Las Casas was at that time favorable to the *encomienda* system, in which Amerindians were assigned as forced labor to Spaniards managing agricultural, pastoral, or mining properties. He himself had many slaves, but in 1514 he underwent a spiritual conversion, renounced his participation in the *encomienda* system, and devoted the rest of his life to denouncing its injustices before the Emperor, the Pope, and in public debate with Juan Ginés de Supúlveda, whose books defended the policies interpreted and carried out by the *encomenderos*.

Sepúlveda argued, first, that the Amerindians were "barbarians, simple, unlettered, and uneducated, brutes totally incapable of learning anything but mechanical skills, full of vices, cruel, and of a kind such that it is advisable they be governed by others,"[56] and secondly, that the Spaniards had a duty to eradicate idolatry and human sacrifices. To these arguments Las Casas replied by asking, in the spirit of Montaigne, Who were the real barbarians? He observed that the vices indicated were found in all societies, that truly monstrous behavior was equally rare in any of them, and that there is no natural hierarchy of peoples. His argument was that all individual humans were alike in being rational, possessing understanding and free choice, and that all are made in the image and likeness of God—that, in short, the entire human race is one.

There were many other highly interesting matters in dispute between them, but what is striking is that the arguments advanced by Las Casas amount to an extension of human empathy, at least two centuries in advance of its time, which resulted not from any reassessment of the facts but from a change of *attitude*, caused in this case by a spiritual conversion. (Another instance of such an extension is the question posed by the last and greatest of the French Enlightenment philosophes, Condorcet, in 1789: "Has not everyone violated the principle of equal rights by calmly depriving half the human race of the right to take part in the formation of the laws?"[57])

Moral diversity, Brandt argues, takes the form of a fundamental moral disagreement when it is exhibited by conflicting attitudes and does not hinge on divergent assessments of the nonmoral facts. But to count as a genuine case, other conditions must be present. People or peoples will disagree in a morally fundamental way if they continue to disagree in their moral judgments under three "idealized" conditions. First, they should, as already stated, be fully aware of the relevant facts. Second, they should view the issues in an impartial and principled or non-self-interested way—that is, they should be willing to universalize their judgments to relevantly similar individuals in relevantly similar situations. And third they should be free from "abnormal" states of mind, such as insanity, fatigue, and depression. The point of positing these conditions is to try to isolate *moral* disagreements from those deriving from empirical beliefs, from bias due to the distorting effects of self-interest, and from cognitive impairments and irrationality. Brandt called the attitudes that people *would have* under these conditions "qualified attitudes"—attitudes that are free of factual disagreement, self-interested bias, and psychological abnormality. The idea is that where these exist, whether actually or potentially, in a given population, and yet people disagree, there is moral diversity.

Despite the paucity of reliable evidence and the difficulties of interpreting it, Brandt wrote that he was inclined "to think there is ultimate ethical disagreement, and that it is well established," but then, rather confusingly, he added that maybe "it is not very important, or very pervasive."[58] There were by the end of the 1960s several valuable studies within the field of "culture and personality," such as Margaret Mead's cross-cultural studies of gender roles and relations, Benedict's comparative study of Japanese and Western culture, and the Whitings' research into different societies' socialization practices. It is, however, only recently that cultural psychologists have begun to amass what Sperber would recognize as "actual data," data of different kinds that, taken together, could in principle help to determine the pervasiveness and importance of moral diversity across societies and cultures.

Consider first the study Richard E. Nisbett and Dov Cohen made of the "culture of honor" they find in the American South.[59] Its methodology is far more pluralistic than that of the earlier studies, appealing to the findings of ethnographers and historians but in turn accumulating a wide array of data by archival, survey, and experimental methods, both in the laboratory and the field—the great bulk of which, they claim, "speaks with a single voice" in favor of their conclusions.[60] As they remark, the typical anthropological "culture of honor" is "a Mediterranean village where the individual lives in a small face-to-face community that he will never leave," where honor "suffuses all social relations" such that a person "sits in the proper pew or not; and his daughter marries well or badly, depending on his honor."[61] Their conception of a culture of honor is more analytically focused and more revealing. They take *honor* to be based not merely on good character but "on a man's strength and power to enforce his will on others." For them, what cultures of honor have in common is that the individual "is prepared to protect his reputation—for probity or strength or both—by resort to violence," and such cultures are likely to develop where "(1) the individual is at economic risk from his fellows and (2) the state is weak or nonexistent and thus cannot prevent or punish theft of property."[62] Such a culture differs from others in that "its members are prepared to fight or even to kill to defend their reputations as honorable men." Hence the importance of the insult and the need to respond to it, for an "insult implies that the target is weak enough to be bullied," and since it is essential to maintain a reputation for strength, "the individual who insults someone must be forced to retract; if the instigator refuses, he must be punished, with violence or even death."[63]

Their study marshals a wide range of evidence that southerners, as compared to northerners—more specifically, whites, not blacks, living in more rural areas and smaller towns—are "more inclined to favor violence when it is for the protection of property, or as a response to an insult, or as a means of socializing children."[64] Thus they have significantly higher homicide rates and specifically where arguments, brawls, and lovers' triangles are concerned rather than felony-related homicides. They have distinctive attitudes toward violence that exhibit a distinctive cycle in which

> arguments lead to affronts that demand retribution. The availability of guns increases the chances that the retribution may be deadly. In addition, the knowledge that the other person may be armed and may begin acting violently may lead to preemptive first strikes. Once conflicts escalate, a man may be more apt to take a first strike as a matter of self-protection before he himself gets shot. At a cultural level, the occurrence of

hundreds of these self-fulfilling prophecies creates a milieu where the threat of violence keeps individuals vigilant (perhaps hypervigilant) in their own defense.[65]

In such a milieu, there are "high costs for backing down from a challenge, *and everyone knows it*. Once the gauntlet has been thrown down, the preemptive first strike may be construed by some as a necessary act of self-defense." And this, the authors suggest, might account for "southern hospitality, politeness, and friendliness" serving to "keep social interactions going smoothly."[66]

They bolster this analysis, based on census and crime reports and attitude surveys, with evidence from laboratory experiments on reactions to direct insults (by college students from the South), which suggests that insults are a much more serious matter for southerners than for northerners, making the affronted southerner feel diminished, with notable physiological effects, and leading to aggressive or domineering behavior to reestablish his masculine status. At the level of collective expression, laws in the South and West allow more freedom to use violence to defend oneself and one's home and property, and there is more support for national defense policies, greater leniency toward domestic violence, more tolerance of corporal punishment in the schools, and a greater willingness to carry out executions. And two revealing field experiments show southern employers and journalists to be markedly more indulgent when faced with believable stories of honor-related violence.

Nisbett and Cohen's explanation of the origins of the honor culture of the South is economy-based. They argue that the southern United States was unique in being settled primarily by people—the so-called Scotch-Irish—who had always been herders and that a herding economy is peculiarly conducive to culture-of-honor tendencies (and indeed, the feuding societies of the world are preponderantly herding societies). Herding economies, they suggest, are conducive to violence because of the inherent risks involved in such economies (as opposed to hunter-gatherer and stable agricultural economies). But whatever the origins of honor cultures,[67] Nisbett and Cohen offer an interesting speculation concerning the mechanisms that thereafter sustain them. Recalling Montaigne's account of the origins of custom's grip, they suggest that once the ideals of the culture of honor "are separated from the initial reasons for their existence and incorporated into gender roles, they may become much more impervious to change. Many patterns of behavior continue because they are defined as things that *a man just does*: he protects his family from threats, he answers serious insults with violence, he spanks his children to discipline them, and he protects his honor and status in the community. Those are just things you have to do."[68] They cite John Reed, who asks, "How do southerners learn that violence is acceptable in some circumstances and not others?" and answers that this "aspect of culture is simply taken in like others. . . . [I]t is absorbed, pretty much without reflection, in childhood. . . ."[69]

Does this case study offer evidence of moral diversity? Does it point to moral attitudes diverging even under the indicated idealized conditions? This is, of course, disputable. The philosophers John Doris and Stephen Stich think that it does, observing that the data shows that southern culture "affects people's judgments, attitudes, emotions, behavior, and even their physiological responses" and that this is the more telling because "contemporary northern and southern Americans might be expected to have more in common—from circumstance to language to belief to ideology—than do, say, Yanomamö and Parisians."[70] Moreover, they write, it is implausible to suggest that the indicated differences are due to southerners' failure to apply their principles impartially, to factual disagreements, or to cognitive impairment or other failures of rationality.

Consider, finally, a grander, indeed classical, cross-cultural theme, long debated by thinkers in different domains, which bears on the issue of moral diversity: namely, the alleged contrast between "Western" individualist and "Eastern" holistic modes of thought and worldviews. Here too cultural psychologists have gone to work and begun to amass interesting and relevant data, and here too we draw on Nisbett, who has brought it together in his recent book, *The Geography of Thought*.[71] Again the findings rely on historical evidence as well as ethnographies, surveys, and laboratory research. For this purpose, "Western" is taken to mean people of European culture and in particular Americans (meaning inhabitants of the United States); and "Eastern" refers specifically to East Asia and in particular China and the countries heavily influenced by its culture, notably Japan and Korea.

The chapter of Nisbett's book entitled "Living Together vs. Going It Alone" deploys a number of familiar contrasts: independence versus interdependence, what he calls "low-context" and "high-context" societies (in the former, individuals and their goals are the focus of attention; in the latter, complex social networks and proscribed social relations are the prime focus). He contrasts as well the Western self as a "bounded, impermeable free agent" and the Eastern as "connected, fluid, and conditional." The wider conclusions of his and others' research are that there are dramatic differences in thought processes in which "social practices promote the worldviews; the worldviews dictate the appropriate thought processes; and the thought processes both justify the worldviews and support the practices."[72] As for the sphere of morals and "values," Nisbett reviews data ranging from linguistic evidence (there is no Chinese word for "individualism") to studies of businesspeople from different cultures (there are differing understandings of what counts as "negotiation") and arrives at the following extremely broad-stroke conclusions:

> East Asians live in an interdependent world in which the self is part of a larger whole; Westerners live in a world in which the self is a unitary free agent. Easterners value success and achievement in good part because they reflect well on the groups they belong to; Westerners value these things because they are badges of personal merit. Easterners value fitting in and engage in self-criticism to make sure that they do so; Westerners value individuality and strive to make themselves look good. Easterners are highly attuned to the feelings of others and strive for interpersonal harmony; Westerners are more concerned with knowing themselves and are prepared to sacrifice

harmony for fairness. Easterners are accepting of hierarchy and group control; Westerners are more likely to prefer equality and scope for personal action. Asians avoid controversy and debate; Westerners have faith in the rhetoric of argumentation in arenas from law to politics to science. [73]

Nisbett qualifies this caricatural, dichotomous picture of culture-defining contrasts, of course. (And is it not, one wonders, itself an instance of his "Western" either-or thinking?) The social psychological characteristics of people raised in very different cultures are, he concedes, far from completely immutable (as assimilating immigrants show), every society "has individuals who more clearly resemble those of other, quite different societies than they do those of their own society; and every individual within a given society moves quite a bit between the independent and interdependent poles over the course of a lifetime—over the course of a day, in fact."[74] Nevertheless, his claim is that the evidence shows that "East and West are in general quite different from each other with respect to a great many centrally important values and social-psychological attributes."[75]

Here once again research appears to confirm commonsense assumptions, even stereotypes, so that the implicit claim is that we can plausibly infer the existence of divergent idealized or "qualified" attitudes and thus moral diversity. But a major problem with Nisbett's book begins with its title but extends to the entire text, which focuses exclusively on accumulating evidence of simplistically characterized cross-cultural contrasts and is entirely silent (apart from the passage just cited)

about inter- and intrasocietal and interpersonal differences. Indeed, apart from very general, and distinctly
arbitrary, observations about the roots of Western thinking in ancient Greece, the book is wholly innocent of
historical and sociological complexity: different national histories, the impact of religions, and the effects
of social class are all absent. Furthermore, the argument is indecisive on the key question of the depth and
stability of these contrasting values and modes of thinking. Are they culturally ingrained or can they be switched
off and on?

It is nevertheless indisputable that such contrasts exist. Consider, for instance, the evidence, some of it cited
by Nisbett, of contrasting business practices (are con-
tracts binding regardless of circumstances? Westerners
tend to say yes, Easterners no) or the ways in which ad-
vertisements appeal to individualist values in the United
States ("Make your way through the crowd") and to col-
lectivist ones in Korea ("We have a way of bringing people closer together"). Or consider a report in the *China
Daily* of an implementation of the norm of filial piety
inconceivable in the West: in Zhejiang Province's Jin-
hua County, villages put up public blackboards on
which elderly parents are supposed to jot down the sum
of money given to them by their children every
month.[76]

~

In this chapter we have considered the formidable difficulties in assessing the extent and nature of moral
diversity. The question is: can they be overcome and, if

so, how and to what extent? Moody-Adams suggests that the obstacles "may be insuperable."[77] She writes that "[c]omparative anthropology provides obvious evidence of cultural variability in moral practices, but why should it be assumed that the moral disagreements sometimes occasioned by that variability are also *fundamental*—rationally irresolvable—moral conflicts?"[78] Do the three examples just cited lend support to such an assumption? Is it plausible to see significant moral diversity within the life of a single individual, in the case of Las Casas; within a single society, as between the northern and southern United States; and across the world, dividing East and West? Can the striking diversities indicated not be seen as deriving from factual disagreements or local differences? Have the cultural psychologists brought us any nearer to an answer?

I am inclined to think that the case of Las Casas does represent a genuine case of a fundamental change of moral attitude in which, first, the scope of moral concern was extended, in favor of universalism, and second, the way it was expressed was radically changed, against "moral imperialism." I am persuaded by William J. Talbott's argument that "there were two crucially important steps in Las Casas's moral development: first, when he changed the interpretation of his moral norms to include the American natives; and second, when he concluded that his culture's norms against cannibalism and idolatry should not be applied to the natives" since he "came to believe that the natives' traditional religious practices, including human sacrifice, were appropriate for them and that it was not wrong for them to engage in their traditional religious practices, even when they were cannibalistic and idolatrous."[79] (For completeness, it should be mentioned that Las Casas did support replacing native slaves with Africans, but later repented and was one of the first Europeans to denounce the African slave trade.[80])

As for the second and third examples, from the cultural psychologists, it is much more debatable that they provide satisfactory answers to Moody-Adams's question. For one thing, it is far from convincing to treat the subjects of their investigations as representatives or embodiments of entire, discrete "cultures" (as we shall see in Chapter 4), especially when these are so grandly and loosely identified as Northern, Southern, Eastern, and Western. Nor have these studies confronted the question of the conditions for Brandt's idealized "qualified attitudes." For example, why should we not believe that southern people have learned that protecting their honor is the way to protect their interests? Why should we not think that they have the factual belief that unless you spank your children, they will become weak and socially inept, so that they must live in an environment in which one should be prepared to be violent to maintain one's status? It is true that the cultural psychologists have amassed a range of different kinds of evidence that appears to speak "with a single voice." But the question remains: what exactly is it evidence of?

Nisbett suggests that the divergences he has documented between "Easterners" and "Westerners" are in "centrally important *values.*" As we will see, the term *values* captures the subjective and intersubjective dimension of morals—what people value and count as worthwhile in their lives and practices as distinct from the norms or rules that they confront and internalize. Nisbett's suggestion of an East/West contrast of centrally important values is a suggestion that has, as we shall see, been raised and sharply contested in the so-called Asian values debate. In the next chapter we will examine the idea of plural and conflicting values, on the assumption that that idea is at the heart of what makes moral relativism attractive.

4

CULTURES AND VALUES

> . . . a cultural series can be traced across all civilized
> nations, branching off at sharply divergent angles. . . .
> [E]ach branch designates increasing and decreasing
> greatness and peaks of perfection of all kinds and many
> of these exclude or limit one another, . . . so that it
> would be misleading to infer that what counts as
> perfection in one nation does so in another.
>
> JOHANN GOTTFRIED VON HERDER[1]

So far we have focused attention on moral *norms*. These
are rules that are external to individuals and internalized by them. They issue injunctions to act or abstain
from acting. Where such norms are operative and effective, they generally guide and shape people's behavior.
When psychologically normal people violate or ignore
them, they generally experience guilt or self-reproach
and others are disposed to punish them, whether infor-
mally (through ostracism, say, or gossip) or formally
through the law. Of course, norms can break down and
loosen their hold, and under certain conditions guilt
and shame can both cease to operate. Under "normal"
conditions, however, most people comply, for a variety
of motives, with the prevailing norms.

In Chapter 2 I asked what role in explaining such
compliance is played respectively by reason, custom, and
nature: to what extent do people reflectively choose to
comply and to what extent are they driven to do so by

external (social) or internal (natural) pressures or some combination of the two? In Chapter 3 I reviewed the difficulties of deciding whether and, if so, how much moral norms diverge across time and space. I now turn to what many believe underlies both the compliance and the divergence: namely, the *values* that people hold, pursue, and live by.

Value Pluralism

The Russian-born Oxford political philosopher and historian of ideas Sir Isaiah Berlin and the great German comparative and historical sociologist Max Weber were, without doubt, the most eloquent twentieth-century exponents of the doctrine that, as Berlin put it, conflicts of values are "an intrinsic, irremovable element in human life"; that life affords "a plurality of values, equally genuine, equally ultimate, above all equally objective; incapable, therefore, of being ordered in a timeless hierarchy, or judged in terms of one absolute standard."[2] This doctrine is often called *value pluralism*. In this chapter I want to ask what we are to mean by *values*, what it means to think of them as plural, and in what ways they conflict. In the next chapter I will ask what support, if any, this doctrine lends to moral relativism.

Value pluralism for Berlin recognizes "the fact that human goals are many, not all of them commensurable, and in perpetual rivalry with one another. To assume that all values can be graded on one scale, so that it is a mere matter of inspection to determine the highest, seems to me to falsify our knowledge that men are free agents, to represent moral decision as an operation which a slide-rule could, in principle, perform." The world we encounter in ordinary experience "is one in which we are faced with choices between ends equally ultimate, and claims equally absolute, the realization of some of which must inevitably involve the sacrifice of others." There is no "*a priori* guarantee" that "a total harmony of true values is somewhere to be found," and indeed, "the very desire for guarantees that our values are eternal and secure in some objective heaven is perhaps only a craving for the certainties of childhood or the absolute values of our primitive past."[3]

The same doctrine was no less dramatically expressed by Max Weber, for whom, in our disenchanted modern world, "the ultimately possible attitudes toward life are irreconcilable, and hence their struggle can never be brought to a final conclusion." Ethics, unlike science, does not yield conclusions on which we can expect to converge, least of all answers to what Tolstoy called "the only question important for us: 'What shall we do and how shall we live?'" Who, Weber asked,

> will take upon himself the attempt to "refute scientifically" the ethic of the Sermon on the Mount? For instance, the sentence, "resist no evil," or the image of turning the other cheek? And yet it is clear, in mundane perspective, that this is an ethic of undignified conduct; one has to choose between the religious dignity which this ethic confers and the dignity of manly conduct which preaches something quite different; "resist evil—unless you be co-responsible for an overpowering evil." According to our ultimate standpoint, the one is the devil and the other the God,

and the individual has to decide which is God and which is the devil. And so it goes throughout all the orders of life.[4]

And, Weber says, not to recognize the significance of this value pluralism for politics is to be "a political infant."[5]

There are several ideas here. Both thinkers suggest that values involve human goals and answers to Tolstoy's question "What shall we do and how shall we live?" Both suggest that they can be ultimate and thus *irreducible*: in at least some, perhaps many, cases, they cannot be reduced to one another or subsumed under some overarching value, such as "utility" or the welfare or happiness of all. Thus, rights can trump the collective good: the protection of basic rights—to a fair trial, for instance—is not to be abandoned for what appears to be in the collective interest. Sometimes values are *incommensurable* and so cannot be ranked higher or lower, or indeed equivalent or equal, on some scale or according to some common metric. As we shall see, we often reject the very idea of measuring or weighing some of the virtues and relations that we value, such as honor and friendship.

Both thinkers suggest that values can be irreconcilable, in several ways. Conflicting values may be *incompatible*: they cannot both be simultaneously pursued and lived by the same individual, who must therefore choose between them, sacrificing one for the other. You cannot simultaneously embrace asceticism and hedonism, nationalism and cosmopolitanism. Sometimes values may be incompatible not only at the individual level but also socially, where the existence of social institutions and structures favoring one cannot coexist with those favoring the other—though you may, as immigrants typically do, try to recreate elements of the world you have lost. And the conflicting values can be *mutually denunciatory*, as in Weber's example, where to take one seriously is to repudiate the other. Both thinkers suggest that recognition of these features of human values is inherent in modernity and that it is a sign of personal maturity.

Weber came to this view, among other routes, via Nietszche. Berlin discerned its roots, among other places, in the thought of Machiavelli, whose originality, he wrote, was to have seen that "there exist at least two sets of virtues—let us call them the Christian and the pagan—which are not merely in practice, but in principle incompatible." The undoubted virtues of "pity, humility, self-sacrifice, obedience" and so on are "incompatible with those social ends which he thinks it natural and wise for men to seek." For if men "practise Christian humility, they cannot also be inspired by the burning ambitions of the great classical founders of cultures and religions; if their gaze is centred upon the world beyond—if their ideas are infected by even lip-service to such an outlook—they will not be likely to give all that they have to an attempt to build a perfect city." Machiavelli, in short, "uncovered an insoluble dilemma" and thereby planted "a permanent question-mark in the path of posterity." For he recognized that "ends, equally ultimate, equally sacred, may contradict each other, that entire systems of value may come into collision without possibility of rational arbitration, and that not merely in exceptional circumstances, as a result of abnormality or accident or error—the clash of Antigone and Creon or in the story of Tristan—but (this was surely new) as part of the normal human situation."[6]

Both Weber and Berlin saw this idea in the thinking of John Stuart Mill, who, despite his surviving commitment to utilitarianism and his undoubted faith in social and individual progress, was, as Berlin interprets him, keenly aware of the multiple "ends of life," of its many-sidedness and irreducible complexity, and believed that "there are no final truths not corrigible by experience" in the sphere of "value judgments and of general outlook and attitude to life."[7] Weber observed that for Mill, if "one proceeds from pure experience, one arrives at polytheism." Weber, like Nietzsche, endorsed this view of "the struggle that the gods of the various orders and values are engaged in." And he cited as an example the impossibility of deciding "scientifically" between "the value of French and German culture; for here too, different gods struggle with one another, now and for all times to come."[8]

The Cultural Turn

This last idea—that value pluralism expresses irreconcilable differences between cultures—has been a massively influential idea, with immense political consequences, to which we must now turn our attention. Value pluralism took a cultural turn in the late eighteenth century, inspired by Romanticism and in reaction to the abstract universalism of the French Enlightenment. The key figure was the German philosopher and poet Johann Gottfried von Herder, dissident pupil of Kant and resident of the polyglot city of Riga (also, as it happens, the birthplace of Isaiah Berlin), home to Germans, Latvians, and

Russians. His thought stands at the opposite pole from that of the Scottish Enlightenment philosopher David Hume, who asked, "Would you know the sentiments, inclinations, and course of life of the Greeks and Romans? Study well the temper and actions of the French and the English: You cannot be much mistaken in transferring to the former *most* of the observations which you have made with regard to the latter. Mankind are so much the same, in all times and places, that history informs us of nothing new or strange in this particular."[9]

Herder believed in *radical differences* of mentalities. These differences were radical in the sense that the standards by which they might be compared were always internal to one or another culture. Herder once remarked: "I do not like comparing at all"[10] and wrote that every nation and culture "bears in itself the standard of its perfection, totally independent of all comparison with that of others."[11] Every nation and every age, he wrote, "has its centre of happiness within itself, just as every sphere has its centre of gravity."[12] There are, he thought, diverse ways of human flourishing: we all believe "that we still now have *parental* and *household* and *human drives* as the Oriental had them; that we can have *faithfulness* and *diligence in art* as the Egyptians possessed them; *Phoenician activeness, Greek love of freedom, Roman strength of soul. . . .*"[13]

Concepts, beliefs, even sensations and the sentiments that underlie morality differ in deep ways from one historical period and one culture to another; and these differences are rooted in and bounded by different languages. Mother Nature has made us all ethnocentric. She has put "tendencies towards diversity in our hearts;

she has placed part of the diversity in a close circle around us; she has restricted man's view so that by force of habit the circle became a horizon, beyond which he could not see nor scarcely speculate."[14] The answer according to Herder is to engage in *holistic interpretation*. This requires you to "go into the age, the clime, the whole history, feel yourself into everything—only now are you on the way to understanding."[15]

Herder's thought lies at the origins of both sociolinguistics and anthropology and was, indeed, a strong influence on Boas (and thus on the subsequent cultural relativism we have considered earlier) and also on Malinowski, who in turn strongly influenced British social anthropology. In fact, Herder also held views that counteracted the more radical implications of his value pluralism. His was a progressive view of history as the realization of "reason" and "humanity." He thought that the mental worlds of other cultures were always accessible through a kind of empathetic understanding. He thought that the infinite cultural variety he discerned was "striving for a unity that lies in all, that advances all" whose name was "understanding, fairness [*Billigkeit*], goodness, *feeling of humanity*,"[16] and which was expressed in all human cultures by numerous different versions of the Golden Rule, Do unto others as you would have them do unto you.

Whereas these universalist residues of the Enlightenment, though central to Herder's thinking, have, however, often been discarded by others, his key idea of conflicting and incommensurable values that are internal to different cultures (which I shall henceforth unfairly label "Herderian") was and remains extraordinarily powerful in its appeal. It was present from the beginning at the heart of modern nationalism—as Weber's remark about the eternal struggle between "the gods" of French and German cultures vividly illustrates. Thus Fichte in his "Thirteenth Address to the German Nation" wrote that it is only in "the invisible peculiarities of nations" that "we can find the guarantee" of their "present and future dignity, virtue, and merit" and that "if these qualities are dulled by mixture and disintegration, there arises from this lack of peculiarity a separation from spiritual nature, and from that there arises the fusion of all in uniform and conjoint ruin."[17] In such words can be heard the authentic tones of culture-based exclusivity that echo, sometimes less and sometimes more harshly, in the voices of successive proponents of nationalism down the decades and across the world until today. The national culture—like the cultures of twentieth-century anthropologists—is typically seen as homogenizing within and to be defended against homogenization without—against assimilation or mongrelization within a cosmopolitan or Westernizing "fusion" of values.

A striking example of this view is to be found in Jomo Kenyatta's book *Facing Mount Kenya*, published in 1938,[18] in which the future founding father of the Kenyan nation insists that "the various sides of Gikuyu life" are "parts of an integrated culture" from which "[n]o single part is detachable; each has its context and is fully understandable only in relation to the whole."[19] This national culture teaches the individual "his mental and moral values and makes him feel it worth while to work and fight for liberty."[20] One essential side of the culture consists in the initiation rites, in particular the custom of clitoridectomy of girls, which is described in vivid and gruesome detail (but executed, Kenyatta maintains, "with the dexterity of a Harley Street surgeon"[21]). This ritual "has been strongly attacked" by "a good many Europeans" who see it as "nothing but a 'horrible' and 'painful' practice, suitable only to barbarians,"[22] whereas "it is the most important custom among the Gikuyu," for these rites are "looked upon as giving a boy or a girl the status of manhood or womanhood in the Gikuyu community."[23] Its abolition, Kenyatta writes, would "destroy the tribal symbol which identifies the age-groups, and prevent the Gikuyu from perpetuating that spirit of collectivism and national solidarity which they have been able to maintain from time immemorial."[24] It is noteworthy that Malinowski, in whose discussion class Kenyatta had studied anthropology at the London School of Economics, wrote the introduction to the book, describing it as "a personal statement of the new outlook of a progressive African" who "presents the facts objectively."[25]

The influence of this Herderian view of culture extends far beyond the traditional forms of nationalism. As Seyla Benhabib has observed,

> much contemporary cultural politics today is an odd
> mixture of the anthropological view of the democratic
> equality of all cultural forms of expression and the
> Romantic, Herderian emphasis on each form's
> irreducible uniqueness. Whether in politics or in policy,
> in courts or in the media, one assumes that each human
> group "has" some kind of "culture" and that the
> boundaries between these groups and the contours of

their cultures are specifiable and relatively easy to depict. Above all, we are told, it is good to preserve and propagate such cultures and cultural differences.[26]

So, for instance, this view of cultures is to be found in much of the thinking that inspires and the discourse that justifies the politics and policies of multiculturalism. It is the patchwork or "mosaic" view of cultures as monochrome unities with sharply defined borders. Even Will Kymlicka, the most liberal of multicultural theorists, whose version of multiculturalism focuses on national minorities, territorially based and sharing a language, holds this view. He does so for the individualist reason that living within one's own culture enhances one's personal freedom. He writes that we should "aim at ensuring that all national groups have the opportunity to maintain themselves as a distinct culture, if they so choose"[27] and that people can only make choices among meaningful options within "a rich and secure cultural structure."[28] But this makes two questionable assumptions: that the world divides neatly into distinct cultures and that everyone needs just one such culture to live a meaningful and free life (and why assume that meaningful choices require a unitary and coherent culture?). If these assumptions are questionable in relation to national minorities, they will be even more so in respect of immigrant groups, upon which the politics of multiculturalism has mainly focused.

Consider the case of the Netherlands, a country famed for its permissiveness and tolerance. The Dutch government made an ambitiously broad commitment to preserve, even promote, a Muslim way of life—or more precisely, one version of a Muslim way of life that prevails in rural and remote areas of the Muslim world and is most at odds with the pluralistic spirit of liberal democracy. It did this, not because of electoral pressures from the majority, but under the influence of well-intentioned policy advisers and leaders of informed opinion. It funded separate schools, housing projects, broadcast media, and community organizations for Muslim immigrants that increased the influence of Muslim leaders who took pride in rejecting Western European values. Holland was seen as an exemplary case of immigrant multiculturalism, but, with terrorism, in particular September 11, 2001, and the radicalization of Muslim immigrants, the dream was shattered. The killing of the filmmaker Theo van Gogh accelerated a crisis of identity politics, turning accommodation into confrontation, so that Holland has become what a recent study describes as the scene of a "collision between Western European and Muslim values."[29]

The authors of that study make two significant observations that relate to our argument. First, they note that the Dutch experience is a "textbook example of the quicksilver character of cultures," since, even after World War II, the Netherlands used to be characterized by "traditional male-female roles; gender segregation in primary schools and in the church on Sundays; fear of nudity and sexuality; physical punishment of children; an ideology of family solidarity over individualism; and immense respect for authority."[30] Secondly, they argue that the origins of the present confrontational clash of values predate the rise of terrorism. That clash is a consequence of the accentuation of cultural identities seen as distinct and

incompatible: for making minorities and multiculturalism "the focal point of public attention and argument
generated a deep-lying suspicion, a belief that Muslim
immigrants wanted to live in their new country but not
be a part of it; a suspicion of divided loyalty that took
root not just at the periphery but at the center of
society—among the most educated, best off, and most
tolerant."[31] For

> the whole thrust of multiculturalism is to accentuate,
> even exaggerate, differences between majority and
> minority and insist on their importance. "Our" way of
> life versus "theirs"; "our" language versus "theirs"; "our"
> religion (or lack of it) versus "theirs"; "our" ideas of
> fairness and respect versus "theirs." One consequence of
> this accentuation of differences is opposition to policies
> to help minorities—opposition piled on top of the
> opposition grounded in prejudice. Another consequence
> is hostility to minorities—hostility piled on top of the
> hostility rooted in prejudice. . . . [B]ringing differences
> of ethnic and religious identity to the fore evokes the
> very exclusionary reactions it is meant to avoid.[32]

Perhaps surprisingly, this same view of cultures is
also at work at the geopolitical level in the hugely influential work of Samuel Huntington, *The Clash of Civilizations and the Remaking of World Order*.[33] Insofar
as the ideas expressed in that book have infiltrated
Western public discourse, it has achieved, to an extent
we cannot yet ascertain, the status of a self-fulfilling
prophecy that bodes ill for the future peace of the
world. These ideas amount to a curious cocktail of

international relations realism and cultural essential-ism. It is hard to mistake the Herderian, indeed Fich-tean echoes in Huntington's preoccupation with "The American Creed" and his worries about its message be-ing dulled by mixture and disintegration.[34] Hunting-ton's view is that in the "emerging world of ethnic conflict and civilizational clash, Western belief in the universality of Western culture suffers three problems: it is false, it is immoral and it is dangerous."[35] So Hun-tington's answer to facing the conflict is that North America and Europe should "renew their moral life, build on their cultural commonality, and develop close forms of economic and political integration to supple-ment their security collaboration in NATO [so that] they could generate a third Euroamerican phase of Western economic affluence and political influence."[36] Domestically this implies resisting the "American mul-ticulturalists," who "wish to create a country of many civilizations, which is to say a country not belonging to any civilization and lacking a cultural core. History shows that no country so constituted can long endure as a coherent society."[37] Huntington's view of the world is "in terms of seven or eight civilizations."[38] He views them as defined by culture and by religion, lumping the two together, indeed for the most part viewing culture in religious terms. Thus he writes that the "central di-viding line" in Europe after the Cold War "is now the line separating the people of Western Christianity, on the one hand, from Muslim and Orthodox people on the other."[39] He argues that the "underlying problem for the West is not Islamic fundamentalism. It is Is-lam."[40] "The West" is characterized by its Christian values, which also, it appears, contrast with China's "Confucian heritage, with its emphasis on authority, order, hierarchy, and supremacy of the collectivity over the individual," which "creates obstacles to democratization."[41]

This last observation of Huntington's indicates a final context in which Herderian cultural essentialism has held sway: namely, the so-called Asian values debate, now largely over, in which the issue in contention was, precisely, the claim that such values favor an alternative, nondemocratic development path and the further claim that they are incompatible with the supposedly "Western" or "European" idea of human rights. At the level of official rhetoric, this has plainly been a self-serving justification for state authoritarianism and the suppression of rights in the name of stability and competitiveness. This has been clearest in the case of Malaysia's prime minister Mahathir Mohamad and, above all, Singapore's Lee Kuan Yew who, condemning the "chaotic and crumbling" societies of the West, declared that Asians have "little doubt that a society with communitarian values where the interests of the society take precedence over that of the individual suits them better than the individualism of America."[42]

It is striking that Lee's argument was decisively challenged and refuted by other Asians: among leaders by Kim Dae Jung, former president of South Korea, and by Lee Teng-Hui, former president of Taiwan—both countries more strongly influenced by Confucianism than Singapore and both scoring relatively well, despite their authoritarian pasts, in regard both to democratic institutions and respect for human rights.[43] Kim Dae

Jung, in an article entitled "Is Culture Destiny? The Myth of Asia's Anti-Democratic Values," argued, indeed, that in some ways the "traditional strengths of Asian society can provide for a better democracy."[44] There are ways of justifying legitimate dissent, government accountability, and the recognition of human rights in distinctively Confucian terms. At the level of the academic discussion of ideas, many scholars have been extensively exploring these ways. One of them is Joseph Chan, who has sought to elaborate a Confucian perspective on human rights on the assumption that different cultures can "justify human rights in their own terms and perspectives," and perhaps an "overlapping consensus" on the norms of human rights may "emerge from self-searching exercises as well as common dialogue."[45] Furthermore, Simon Leys's translation of *The Analects of Confucius* suggests that there are Confucian duties of *disobedience* to rulers that the traditions of imperial and state Confucianism has obliterated.[46] In short, it is clear that here too the idea that values come in stable, integrated, mutually exclusive configurations called "cultures" is seriously mistaken in accounting for how the world works and is both retrograde and dangerous as a guide to political action.

Metaphors for Culture

How, then, should we think about cultures and about how they relate to values? Contrast the Herderian/Fichtean picture we have been considering with the writer Salman Rushdie's response to the more vociferous Muslim critics of his novel *The Satanic Verses*. These critics believed that intermingling with a different culture will undoubtedly weaken and ruin their own. I am of the opposite opinion. *The Satanic Verses* celebrates hybridity, impurity, intermingling, the transformation that comes of new and unexpected combinations of human beings, cultures, ideas, politics, movies, songs. It rejoices in mongrelization and fears the absolutism of the Pure. *Mélange,* hotchpotch, a bit of this and a bit of that is *how newness enters the world.* It is the great possibility that mass migration gave the world, and I have tried to embrace it. *The Satanic Verses* is for change by fusion, change by conjoining. It is a love-song to our mongrel selves. . . .

I was born an Indian, and not only an Indian, but a Bombayite—Bombay, most cosmopolitan, most hybrid, most hotchpotch of Indian cities. My writing and thought have there been as deeply influenced by Hindu myths and attitudes as Muslim ones. . . . Nor is the West absent from Bombay. I was already a mongrel self, history's bastard, before London aggravated the condition.[47]

Jeremy Waldron, who quotes this passage in a paper entitled "Minority Cultures and the Cosmopolitan Alternative," gives the following account of what life à la Rushdie can be like for a cosmopolitan: "Though he may live in San Francisco and be of Irish ancestry, he does not take his identity to be compromised when he learns Spanish, eats Chinese, wears clothes made in Korea, listens to arias by Verdi sung by a Maori princess on Japanese equipment, follows Ukrainian politics, and practises Buddhist meditation techniques."[48] Waldron denies that "all people *need* their rootedness in the particular culture in which they and their ancestors were reared, in the way that they need food, clothing and shelter."[49] But he also makes the stronger claim that "the hybrid lifestyle of the true cosmopolitan is in fact the only appropriate response to the modern world in which we live"—that it is "this limitless diversity of character— Rushdie's *mélange* or hotchpoteh—that makes it possible for each of us to respond to a multifaceted world in new and creative ways."[50]

A new wave of contemporary anthropologists, critical of the essentializing and exoticizing views of culture they see as predominant in the discipline hitherto, have pursued the same theme. So, for example, the influential literary theorist James Clifford writes that culture is "contested, temporal and emergent," "a form of personal and collective self-fashioning"[51]: it consists in "hybrid and subversive forms of cultural representation, forms that prefigure an inventive future."[52] Critics, notably the anthropologist Jonathan Friedman, observe that this conception of cultures is typical of a privileged, world-traveling elite who "are the producers of globalizing representations of the world, understandings that challenge the very existence of the nation state and proclaim a new post-national era at the same time as fragmentation and cultural conflict are more pervasive than ever at the lower levels of the system" with indigenous movements in pursuit of roots.[53] Let us call the Rushdie-Clifford kind of view the *kaleidoscope* view of culture. Its contrast with the patchwork or mosaic view is evident, as is the opposition between the conceptions of "identity" and "the self" that each presupposes: namely, that between a communitarian "embedded" self whose identity is there to be discovered or rediscovered, and a postmodern "self-inventing" self whose identity is yet to be created and re-created anew from an increasing variety of cultural elements available from around the globe.

From within sociology another metaphor for culture has been proposed.[54] Arguing that a culture "is not a unified system that pushes action in a consistent direction," Ann Swidler has suggested that it is more like a "'tool-kit' of resources," of "symbols, stories, rituals, and world-views, which people may use in varying configurations to solve different kinds of problems."[55] This suggestion—inspired by a study of "ghetto culture" in American cities—was made in reaction to the then-dominant view of culture in American sociology, deriving from Talcott Parsons (another legatee of the Herderian view), according to which social systems realize "core values," which are provided by cultural traditions that shape actions by defining what people want. Instead Swidler proposes, convincingly, that people have all kinds of different wants and pursue innumerable ends in different situations, but they do so with a restricted and distinctive set of skills and habits that constitute their "cultural equipment."[56] Real cultures, she writes, consist in "diverse, often conflicting symbols, rituals, stories, and guides to action"[57] that encourage and reinforce people's ways of acting. Indeed, "people will come to value ends for which their cultural equipment is well suited."[58] So, for example, ghetto youth, who expertly "read" signs of friendship and loyalty and recognize threats to "turf" and dignity, will come to value group loyalty more than individual achievement, not because of the values of their culture but because "the cultural meanings and social skills necessary for playing *that* game well would require drastic and costly cultural retooling."[59] When lives are "unsettled," religious or political ideologies can provide new cultural models that induce new "habits of action," new "styles of self, relationship, co-operation, authority, and so forth."[60] In more settled times, culture's effects are harder to disentangle, since it functions to reinforce and refine established ways of acting. Swidler cites as one example the small role played in young women's career plans and family choices by values and plans as opposed to their immediate situations: "a first job which works out, or a boyfriend who does not." Another example is how French workers, "faced with the threats of early industrialism, drew on traditions of corporate organization to construct an ideology of radical socialism."[61]

Yet another metaphor for culture has been proposed by the philosopher Mary Midgley. Cultures, she writes, "do differ, but they differ in a way that is much more like that of climatic regions or ecosystems than it is like the frontiers drawn with a pen between nation states. They shade into one another. And in our own day there is such a pervading and continuous and all-pervading cultural interchange that the idea of separateness holds no water at all."[62] The idea of cultures as separate social monoliths is "utterly unreal and unhistorical," deriving from earlier anthropologists who were in search of uncontaminated objects of study and from the unreal histories generated by mythmakers—cultural entrepreneurs—engaged in unifying groups imaginatively by making their customs look sacred and unchangeable. As for the idea of "Western" culture, embraced by Huntington, she observes that this "has been built up out of endless contributions from Greeks, Jews, Romans, Celts, and in later years from practically every country in the world, and still contains a rich confusion of uncombined elements from all these sources." (She might have cited Claude Lévi-Strauss's observation that all cultures are "the result of a mishmash, borrowings, mixtures that have occurred, though at different rates, since the beginning of time."[63]) Midgley's metaphor is rich in implications. First, there are no sharp boundaries around cultures, which shade into one another, as any seasoned traveler knows. Second, the boundaries are porous: cultures are open systems, whose internal functioning is continuously affected by the impact of outside forces, from near and afar. And third, where are we to draw the boundaries? We sometimes talk about subcultures—as, for example, with "ghetto culture"—but at what level are they supposed to start? And how large is a culture anyway? The very view of cultures as social monoliths with clear boundaries is the view of interested parties, anthropologists from without and mythmakers from within.

These various images of cultures, all proposed in criticism of the mosaic view, capture important truths but are, like analogies, imperfect. The postmodern *kaleidoscope* view certainly captures the eclecticism and rootlessness that increasingly many people experience and value in their lives. But Friedman is right to suggest that this view results from the partial perspective of the social class of frequent flyers, as opposed to "so many working class border-crossers in the world" (he is thinking, I presume, of illegal immigrants) who are "less interested in celebrating their border crossing than in avoiding precisely the borders which are so dangerous in their lives."[64] And Waldron certainly goes far too far in claiming that "the hybrid life of the true cosmopolitan is in fact the only appropriate response to the modern world in which we live." The prevalence and appeal of communitarian allegiances to localities, regions, and nations across the world are far too significant to be so airily dismissed.

The *toolkit* metaphor, by viewing culture as a set of resources, restores agency to individuals, seeing them as "active, sometimes skilled users of culture" pursuing "strategies of action." These are "ways of organizing action which need not be consciously devised to attain a goal," but "might allow one to reach several different life goals."[65] Examples are depending on a network of kin and friends or relying on selling one's skills in a market. What this view altogether misses, and fails to account for, however, is the lived experience of the sheer facticity of culture. That is what Montaigne meant by the grip of custom and what Durkheim meant when he wrote of morality as both constraining and attracting us, imposing obligations, commitments, and loyalties, and fear and awe in face of what is seen as sacred.

The *ecosystem* view is effective in demystifying the holistic interpretations of cultures to which this experience easily leads, by focusing on causal flows, networks, and open, interconnecting systems. (Another metaphor with similar implications is an epidemiological one, in which cultural "memes" spread and cluster as if by contagion.) What is missing here is precisely what the *kaleidoscope* view emphasizes and applauds: namely, the creative and inventive nature of cultural change, in which cultures endlessly generate newness out of materials inherited from the past. In a kaleidoscope, however, the patterns are random and the elements unchanging. By contrast, the meaningfulness of the elements of culture—of ideas, beliefs, symbols, rituals, artistic styles, myths, stories, jokes, and so on—marks their distinctness from the elements with which meteorology and climatology are concerned. They come in traditions in which both the elements and the patterns they form are mutually constitutive. And where these are living traditions, both elements and patterns are perpetually being transformed into something new.

These metaphorical views of culture taken together constitute a significant improvement upon the Herderian picture of cultures as integral unities embodying radical differences between conflicting values. We should see cultures rather as looser or tighter clusterings of customs and practices of varying dimensions, coming from home and abroad, which some seek, more or less successfully, to render sacred by imposing unity and boundaries. Joseph Raz, the Oxford legal philosopher, has written that it is "in the interest of every person to be fully integrated in a cultural group"[66]; but this seems unconvincing—unless "integrated" covers the whole range from hyperactive involvement to outright antagonism.[67] People identify with and are identified as belonging to multiple culturally defined groups—local, national, ethnic, religious, and countless others—and they relate to them in multiple ways. In any such group there will always be, whether openly or secretly, those who strongly and fully identify, but there will also always be, openly or secretly, uncertain identifiers, ambivalent identifiers, intermittent identifiers, quasi-identifiers, semi-identifiers, cross-identifiers, nonidentifiers, ex-identifiers, and anti-identifiers. They forge their lives out of cultural resources that are increasingly global, making choices under the constraints of the objective opportunities they face and the skills and habits they acquire from what we call their "culture," whose constraining and attractive pressures they may experience as real.

But does that mean that we should also do so when engaged in explanation? Perhaps, after all, *culture* (as a noun) is an unsatisfactory analytical category and needs further deconstruction, for the reason that the anthropologist Adam Kuper suggests: that treating it as a single system inhibits analysis of the variables it packs together and the factors that in turn explain them. Perhaps, in other words, "[r]eligious beliefs, rituals, knowledge, moral values, the arts, rhetorical genres, and so on should be separated out from one another rather than bound together into a single bundle labeled culture. . . . [I]f the elements of a culture are disaggregated, it is usually not difficult to show that the parts are separately tied to specific administrative arrangements, economic pressures, biological constraints, and so forth."[68] Kuper cites another anthropologist, Eric Wolf, concluding that a culture is "better seen as a series of processes that construct, reconstruct, and dismantle cultural materials, in response to identifiable determinants."[69] And Michele Moody-Adams observes that "there is no conception more mystical and unreflective than the doctrine of cultural integration, along with its usual companion, the assumption that beliefs and values of 'traditional' or 'primitive' societies must be *more* integrated than those of any other."[70] Perhaps, in sum, we would all be better off if we henceforth restricted use of the term *culture* to its adjectival and adverbial forms.

It is an unlikely prospect, for the Herderian holistic impulse dies hard, among social scientists as well as the rest of us: the impulse, that is, to see entire cultures as incarnating values that diverge and sometimes clash. Consider once more the case of the Netherlands. The authors of the study mentioned earlier write of being struck by

> the collision between West European and Muslim values. On some points they have not merely different but diametrically opposing convictions: what West Europeans believe is right, Muslims believe is wrong; what Muslims believe is right, Western Europeans believe is wrong. . . . From a West European perspective, Muslim men dominate Muslim women. They do not have the same freedom as Muslim men to live the lives they wish to live—to pursue the career of their choosing; to go out when and with whom they wish; to be equal in status with their husband within the family. Again, from a West European perspective, Muslim children are brought up in an authoritarian, punitive, insular way. By contrast, from a Muslim perspective, Western European women are not given the respect they deserve; their embodiment of the family honor is not acknowledged; the dangers of sexual freedom are not taken into account. Again from a Muslim perspective, Western European children are not given the discipline they

need. Two ideas of what is right and what is wrong—two ideas that are not only different but in conflict.[71]

The problem with this is not only the undiscriminating categories (one geographical, or rather geopolitical, the other religious) individuating entire cultures. Notice that in the above passage what we are given is each side's stereotyping "perspective" on the other. The claim, however, is that what divides them is their respective *values,* as though the stereotypes were *true.* It is, of course, true that there are significant differences in *practices* among the Dutch, on the one hand, and Muslim immigrants, on the other, of men vis-à-vis women and parents vis-à-vis children. But that is no reason for concluding that all or most members of each population share the same *values* (equated here with convictions, beliefs, and ideas). To see why this is so, we need, finally, to ask what values are.

Values

Values is a term widely used but rarely analyzed.[72] Values are *subjective* (in the next chapter I shall ask whether they may also be objective). They emerge in our consciousness when we reflect on how to justify our choices. They are distinct from preferences, which they underlie, and from tastes. The values we subscribe to or cherish or live by or believe in are ways of characterizing what we care about: what we think makes what we prefer when we choose important or worthwhile. They are the rationales for our choices (which is not to say that we choose our values; we may find them inescapable). What we *say* are our values is not always the best guide to what they really are: we may be deceiving others (for instance, social scientists investigating our values) or ourselves. And of course, we don't consistently "live up to" our values, but if the values we claim to believe in diverge too much from the choices we make, there is reason to doubt that they are indeed our values. They need not be mutually consistent and fully integrated into a coherent plan of life—you may be a wayward person or a *flâneur* and have your values—but if they become too random one may again doubt that they are really your *values* (rather than your impulses or passing whims).

Values are also *abstract*, but they differ in their degree of abstractness. At their most abstract or generic or thin they generate little disagreement. At their thinnest, values are least informative about what people care about. So, for example, both Dutch and immigrant Muslim men will value respect, but that tells us nothing about what they mean by respect. Similarly, politicians will, we may presume, value peace, prosperity, democracy, and so on, and individuals happiness, love, and friendship, but knowing that is to know nothing of what they care about in making the choices they make. (Of course, not everyone adheres to even these values; most do but interpret their meaning differently. Both Quakers and the Mafia, after all, value friendship.) Values can be thinner or thicker. Those that are thicker—such as family honor or equality of opportunity—are closer to specifying what people in fact take to be worthwhile about the practices, activities, relationships, and policies that they prefer. The thicker the values—the more you need to know of the context to understand what they mean to those doing the valuing—the more plural they will be. The "thinner" the values, the less will differences in their interpretation be apparent.

To speak of people's values is to speak of the weightier considerations that move people to choose the way they live and what they prefer. Their values make sense to them over time of the choices they make. They may not always tell the truth about why they value what they value, to others or themselves; but to count truly as their values, they will be thicker rather than thinner, more rather than less stable, more rather than less integrated with other values in their lives. Seeing this is to see why it is mistaken to see "Westerners" and Muslim immigrants as populations divided by contrasting sets of shared values. What divides them is contrasting norms and practices—in marriage and gender relations and in child-rearing, for example—and they engage in these for a variety of motives, which can change over time. Sometimes they engage in these practices out of mere habit or for fear of violating conventional norms. Sometimes they do so because of values they hold, and among these will be sincerely held convictions or beliefs or ideas. People conform to prevailing norms to maintain or enhance their status in their communities, or to assert their power, or to preserve memories of their previous lives or those of their parents, or for reasons of identity—that is, to mark their distinctiveness from others—or because they place a high value on conforming, or perhaps because, like Montaigne, they reason that doing so is the best path to a peaceable life. In short, even where people engage in the same practices, they will do so for a multitude of reasons, including a plurality of values.

According to the doctrine of value pluralism, with

which this chapter began, values are not only plural but conflicting. Sometimes this is straightforward and simply means that there is a conflict over priorities: two goods are desired and you can't have both. You decide to work less hard, valuing your health more than increasing your income. The government, in the context of a terrorist threat, views national security as more important than certain civil liberties. Such conflicts are often described in the language of "trade-offs": more of X for less of Y, more guns for less butter. Often too we talk of "weighing" the values that conflict in such choices in order to determine which, in any given situation, we see as the more important.

It is not, however, always appropriate to think and speak of priority conflicts in the language of trade-offs or in terms of weighing, on the assumption that there is some common currency or scale against which the values of alternative outcomes can be measured and compared. In the language of Kant, we think that some goods are "beyond price," such as human life, and this idea is asserted in official documents, such as charters of human rights and civil constitutions and in speeches by politicians and clergymen. We resist the idea that we can value how much a person's life is worth and whether one person's life is worth more than another's. Yet there is more than a little pretense here, for we expect medical administrators to ration scarce resources and hospital doctors to make decisions that require such calculations in the interests of fairness and sound public policy. Indeed, such calculations are made on a routine basis by policy makers and administrators in the fields of health, industrial safety, transport, and urban planning, by private companies in the costing of safety features, and by insurance companies. The French government maintains tree-lined boulevards at the cost of a predictable number of road accidents per year. In short, we rely on others to take on the burden of assessing how many lives the various goals we value are worth, though the burden is lessened for them by treating such lives as statistical (and for us by knowing nothing or little about the bases for their decisions). We elect politicians and pay administrators to do the dirty work of trading off our health, safety, and sometimes our lives for economic growth, profitability, administrative efficiency, and tree-lined boulevards.

There are, nevertheless, values—call them *incommensurable*—that resist cost-benefit analysis, where the very idea of measuring in order to compare the values of alternative outcomes seems inappropriate. If you were to assess the value of a particular friendship in relation to a sum of money or the pleasures of new acquaintances, or if you ask how much trouble or discomfort maintaining a loving relationship is worth, you may thereby show that the friendship or love is nonexistent or over, or that you have an impoverished or debased understanding of them. We would be shocked if a person with a sick relative set a limit on how much it was worth spending on medical resources to keep that relative alive. (Of course, devotion in such cases is not limitless or divorced from interests. At a certain point uncalculating devotion to a friend becomes pathological and unjust, a case of servile dependence or exploitation, and a friend who expects or demands such devotion is a bad friend. At a certain point those looking after a sick relative must consider the consequences of their declining resources on, say, the education or health of their children.) And we think that certain activities and relationships should be kept apart from the invasions of the market.

What is at issue here are those commitments or allegiances that resist the calculating attitude that the notions of *trade-off* and *weighing* imply. Here the religious metaphor of *sacrifice* appears more apposite (though these three terms are often used, especially by economists, as equivalent in meaning). We are dealing with all-or-nothing commitments and devotion that exclude bargaining and balancing. It was this kind of value conflict that Jean-Paul Sartre had in mind when, in *Existentialism and Humanism,* he cited the case of a young man torn between staying with his bereaved mother and leaving to fight for the Free French.[73] Value conflicts of this kind are sometimes seen as involving tragic choices, where there is no way to avoid performing a bad action and where the loss involved and the wrong committed remain uncanceled.

Incommensurable values are values we view as *sacred* in the sense specified by Emile Durkheim. We treat practices and relationships as sacred when they are set apart as incommensurable with all others: when we devote ourselves to furthering and maintaining them without calculating the loss involved, by not measuring the benefits against the costs, and by the embarrassment or outrage we feel when others do so. Sacred values, in this sense, can be religious or secular. They can be held unquestioningly as a matter of faith or in a fully rational and reflective manner. They can be particularist, expressing our allegiance to a religion or class or community or nation, or universalist, as when we seek to protect human rights and the inviolability of persons, for example, against being tortured.

It is values of this kind that Berlin and Weber were thinking of when speaking of irreconcilable value conflict (thus Weber cites the clash between Christian pacifism and the code of military honor and Berlin cites Antigone and Tristan). Here, if one must make a choice where such values are at stake, they cannot be "weighed" or "traded off" against one another to decide which has priority, and there is no further value that can be appealed to that will resolve the conflict. One can only choose by appealing to one of them. It is here, where our commitments seem to be deepest and our willingness to defend them the most intransigent, that value pluralism seems to come closest to moral relativism.

5

THE UNIVERSAL AND THE RELATIVE

Relativism and devaluation of common sense are . . .
two sides of the same coin. Each follows from the
attempt to naturalize the human being that characterizes
the human sciences. Interpreting his actions, beliefs,
feelings as being primarily the effects of psychological,
biological, or socio-cultural forces, they are not
interested in the reasons he might give for such actions,
beliefs, or feelings.   RAYMOND BOUDON[1]

The journey down the road to moral relativism begins
from the observation of the facts of diversity. As an observer you note that there are many moralities. More
precisely, as we saw in Chapter 3, moral norms and systems of such norms are seen as diverging across time
and space, in both content and scope of application. And
as we saw in Chapter 4, what people value in their practices and the conduct of their lives diverges both within
and across what we call cultures, sometimes incommen-
surably. The relativistic turn comes when you transfer
these observations into the first-person perspective of a
moral agent—you are now a person with moral views
and making moral judgments—and you conclude that
therefore there is no one true morality but many, and
that no value perspective is privileged over others, and
none from which all can be evaluated, and so you conclude that your judgments apply only to adherents of
your morality.

The first thing to notice is that the *therefore* in the last sentence is entirely misleading. There is no logical entailment here: the relativist conclusion does not follow inexorably from the observations of factual diversity. Indeed, until the nineteenth century few even contemplated drawing this conclusion. Pascal wrote that "what is truth on one side of the Pyrenees is error on the other" and "three degrees of latitude reverse all jurisprudence; a meridian decides the truth."[2] But it never occurred to him to suppose that the truths of Christianity might be limited in scope. "Mahomet," he wrote, "does not prophesy; Jesus prophesies." For no religion "other than ours has taught that man is born in sin, no sect of philosophers has said it: none has therefore spoken the truth."[3]

Ever since the discoveries at the time of Montaigne, awareness of cross-cultural differences has become ever more vivid and involving, but these were widely seen in the West, even until the end of colonialism, within the framework that opposed the less to the more civilized peoples. Today many people accept the facts about diversity while remaining firmly absolutist and objectivist in their moral views and judgments—among their number Pope Benedict and Allan Bloom, with whose denunciations of moral relativism this book began.

The Pope views science and "the modern image of the world it has created" as seeming to "exclude from reality the basic vision of the Christian faith." While not wishing "to impose on others that which they do not understand," he expects that others "will at least respect the consciences of those who allow their reason to be guided by the Christian faith." From the Pope's standpoint, only the Creator "can establish values that are grounded in the essence of humankind and that are inviolable. The existence of values that cannot be modified by anyone is the true guarantee of our freedom and human greatness; in this fact, the Christian faith sees the mystery of the Creator and the condition of man, who was made in God's image."[4]

As for the late Professor Bloom, it was obvious that "the fact that there have been different opinions about good and bad in different times and places in no way proves that none is true or superior to others." For the nonreligious Bloom, disciple of the philosopher and intellectual father of American neoconservatism, Leo Strauss, men

> live more truly and fully in reading Plato and Shakespeare than at any other time, because they are participating in essential being and are forgetting their accidental lives. . . . The real community of man, in the midst of all the self-contradictory simulacra of community, is the community of those who seek the truth, of the potential knowers, that is, in principle, of all men to the extent that they desire to know. But, in fact, this includes only a few, the true friends, as Plato was to Aristotle, at the very moment they were disagreeing about the nature of the good. Their common concern for the good linked them; their disagreement about it proved that they needed one another to understand it. . . . This, according to Plato, is the only real friendship, the only real common good.[5]

I cite these two examples, not for their representativeness but to illuminate, by contrast, what it is that motivates many people to think it natural to move toward relativist conclusions. For them, scientific and "modern" thinking does indeed exclude from reality not just Christian but all religious faith. They do not expect such faith to "guide" their reason or establish "grounds" for their values. Rather, they seek rational grounds for those values. Nor do they understand how there could be "true or superior" opinions about good and bad, let alone *knowledge* about "the nature of the good," and they can make little sense of phrases like "essential being" and "the only real common good." We live, it is often said, in a "post-metaphysical age" in which our moral views are "without foundations." Or rather (which is to say the same thing) there are too many foundations. For, as Anthony Appiah understates the case, in real life "judgments about right and wrong are intimately tied up with metaphysical and religious belief and with beliefs about the natural order. And these are matters about which agreement may be difficult to achieve."[6]

Moreover, those whose views do rest on religious or metaphysical foundations may disagree about moral issues, so what is the probability that any one denomination or school of thought will have attained knowledge of the truth, and how, lacking belief in such foundations, would one know? And so it seems entirely natural to wonder what authority any given set of moral norms can claim and on what basis we can arrive at our value judgments. Thus we arrive at the idea, explored in Chapter 2, that the answer is that the authority is *social* and the basis emotional; that custom is indeed lord of all and that what we call our reasoning in matters of morals is but a mere coloring of local tribal customs, calculated, as Westermarck thought, to give moral values an objectivity they do not possess. This movement of thought has found sustenance in the context of multiculturalism. It is also sustained by identity politics, which encourages attitudes of exclusivity and pride and calls for respect and the recognition of collective identities. But such respect tends to discourage both criticism and self-criticism. Moody-Adams, observing this connection, asks: "What respect for culture, or for the people who accept a culture, can possibly reside in the relativist's conception of culture as principally a shield against criticism? To view those who accept another culture as so fundamentally 'other' that they cannot engage in reasonable moral inquiry is to see them as less than fully human. In short, the notion that subjecting unfamiliar practices to external criticism fails to respect unfamiliar cultures simply will not stand up to careful scrutiny."[7]

If these are the considerations that draw people toward moral relativism, we must next ask what can lead them away from it. How, in a postmetaphysical and foundationless world, can one justify subscribing to universal moral norms and values, that is, norms and values that apply to all human beings in relevantly similar circumstances? That is the first of two questions I shall address in this final chapter, and in doing so I shall suggest that there are two promising approaches to answering it, one in the spirit of Kant, the other in the spirit of Aristotle. Once it has been addressed, we can turn to the second question, namely, what scope remains for a relativistic approach within the moral domain?

The Moral Domain (2)

In order to consider both questions, we need to return to the question of how to define the moral domain, something I earlier attempted in a provisional way. I offered a very broad and loose definition, suggesting that moral norms cover matters of importance in people's lives where they are faced with distinguishing right from wrong. Such norms are directed at promoting good and avoiding evil, at encouraging virtue and discouraging vice, at avoiding harm to others and promoting their well-being or welfare. In general, they are concerned with the interests of others or the common interest rather than just with the individual's self-interest, and they are distinct from the rules of etiquette, law, and religion (though the conduct they require may overlap with what these require). I also suggested that what counts as "moral" is disputed and that the dispute matters. We now need to see why.

I first introduced the provisional definition just cited as an account of moral norms, but as we saw in Chapter 4, morality at its broadest encompasses both norms and values: both rules that impose obligations, on the one hand, and values, or conceptions of the good, on the other. Durkheim captured this duality when he characterized morality as incorporating both rules imposing obligations and ends that are "desired and desirable": "moral reality," he wrote, "always presents simultaneously these two aspects which cannot be isolated empirically."[8] No act, he wrote, "has ever been performed out of duty alone; it has always been necessary for it to appear in some respect as good."[9] This duality has a long history within philosophy, distinguishing "the right" from "the good" as elements of morality in the broad sense and debating which has priority over the other, which comes first and shapes the other. Here the distinction is between rules that implement and values that express morality as broadly defined in the previous paragraph.

But there is another traditional way of marking this distinction. "The moral" can also be distinguished from "the ethical." This latter way (which descends from Hegel's distinction between *Moralität* and *Sittlichkeit*) involves postulating a different and narrower sense of "moral" that derives from Kant. In this view, morality denotes something that is both more severe and more abstract; and it is seen as applying anywhere and everywhere. It directs attention to the duties or obligations I have to other human beings viewed, from the standpoint of justice, as possessors of rights. The ethical, by contrast, refers to the values and ideals that inhere in one or another specific way of life—and these will, of course, be multiple and sometimes mutually incompatible. Ronald Dworkin, the legal theorist, captured the core of this distinction when he wrote that "ethics includes convictions about which kinds of lives are good or bad for a person to lead, and morality includes principles about how a person should treat other people."[10]

The Core of Narrow Morality

This narrow sense of morality is the focus of Kant's philosophy: for Kant a moral principle indicating what is right and wrong is one that moral agents could will as a universal law. In the same spirit the philosopher

Thomas Scanlon, who focuses on this narrow sense of morality, holds that if a moral norm is to be valid it must be justifiable such that *no one* could reasonably reject it. The key idea here is that "what we owe to each other" (the title of his book[11]) is *justification*. Deciding what is right and wrong requires making a judgment about what others could or could not reasonably reject. Justifiability to others is the key to moral motivation and "must be recognized in, and shape, any morally defensible form of life."[12]

This key idea of justifiability is also at the center of the universalistic moral theory of Karl-Otto Apel, the German philosopher, and Jürgen Habermas, the German sociologist-philospher (a theory that Habermas has considerably modified over the years and that he used to call "discourse ethics" but now calls "discourse morality")—a theory that "defends a morality of equal respect and solidaristic responsibility for everybody."[13] The original motivating idea behind this theory was that in the very practice of human communication, or "rational discourse," there is implicit the commitment to mutual justification among persons on a free and equal basis in unrestricted deliberation. The central idea is what Habermas calls "the discursive principle," according to which only those norms can claim validity that could meet with the agreement of all those concerned, in their capacity as participants in a practical discourse: for a norm to be valid, "the consequences and side-effects of its observance for the satisfaction of each person's particular interests must be acceptable to all."[14] Habermas criticizes Kant for supposing, as a child of the eighteenth century, that "in making moral judgments each individual can project himself into the situation of everyone else *through his own imagination.*" In today's world, "when the participants can no longer rely on a transcendental preunderstanding grounded in more or less homogeneous conditions of life and interests, the moral point of view can only be realized under conditions of communication that ensure that *everyone* tests the acceptability of a norm, implemented in a general practice, also from the perspective of his own understanding of himself and of the world."[15]

Habermas criticizes Kant for relying on his own imagination and extends this critique to contemporary moral philosophers (such as Scanlon and John Rawls) who propose universalistic theories of normative validity by engaging in reasoning and hypothetical thought experiments. His case is that "nothing better prevents others from perspectivally distorting one's own interests than actual participation"[16] and so "the justification of norms requires that real discourse be carried out, and this cannot occur in a strictly monological form, i.e. in the form of a hypothetical process of argumentation occurring in the individual mind."[17] Scanlon replies that "while interaction with others plays a crucial role in arriving at well-founded moral opinions, reaching a conclusion about right and wrong requires making a judgment about what others could or could not reasonably reject. . . . The agreement of others . . . when it occurs does not settle the matter."[18] Aside from this disagreement, what is clear is that both sides are seeking a universalistic basis for assessing the norms governing actual social practices and for condemning some of them: as Scanlon writes, "[s]exual practices and family systems that involve demeaning or enslaving others, for example, are morally excluded."[19] They are both also seeking a basis for selecting norms that, as Habermas writes, "are capable of commanding universal agreement—for example, norms expressing human rights."[20]

Where they differ is that Habermas and those who follow him offer a radically democratic agenda for the actual implementation of "practical discourses" in which, in the social philosopher Seyla Benhabib's words, all who are affected by the consequences of norms and normative institutional arrangements can "be participants in the discourse through which the norms are adopted."[21] Of course, such discourse may "begin with the presumption of respect, equality and reciprocity between the participants," but as Benhabib observes, without actual interaction, "we cannot know what such respect requires or entails in the face of deep cultural conflicts; while some of us may consider certain practices and judgments an affront to human dignity, others may consider our evaluations a species of ethnocentric imperialism."[22] And she cites the example, discussed above in Chapter 2, of the Indian practice of suttee, or widow-burning, and that of the wearing of the veil by Muslim girls. How can one assess the justifiability of these practices without discovering whether they can be justified to all those concerned?

To many nonphilosophers this disagreement about real versus hypothetical discourses to ascertain the justifiability of social practices may seem recondite, even nitpicking. They will argue that Habermas's democratic ideal looks hopelessly unrealistic, since most actual societies are so immensely far removed from the kind of democratic participation he has in mind. But that is a mistake, for there are two striking ways in which ethnographic material can have a bearing on these issues. One is to inquire what cross-cultural study of all the available evidence about a given practice might reveal about that practice's justifiability. It can enable us to *reconstruct* the bases for potential agreement about legitimate norms across cultural boundaries. Of course, the practice must be carefully selected in order to avoid the problems we have explored earlier. It should be a practice generally accepted in widely different societies as norm-governed, not one laid down from on high, in constitutions and the like, by ruling elites, or one embodying the ideals and aspirations of religious prophets or sects; and we need to avoid cultural bias by focusing on what can plausibly be seen as the *same* practice across different contexts. Existing comparative studies of the extent to which human rights and freedoms, such as the freedom of expression, are practiced across the world typically begin with "Western" assumptions about, say, individual responsibility and what counts as democracy; and not surprisingly most "non-Western" societies score bad grades. We need studies of diverse local instances of the same practice that could reveal an "overlapping consensus" (to borrow John Rawls's phrase) about the norms that legitimate them.

That is why the political scientist–anthropologist Alison Renteln's case study of "retribution tied to proportionality"[23] is so interesting in this connection. She begins with the assumption that the principle of retribution (that is, recompense for, or requital of, evil done) may be universal, citing a range of scholars of comparative morality in various domains, suggesting just this.

Retribution implies some notion of equivalence or proportionality. Of course, "what constitutes equivalence between crimes and punishments generally varies cross-culturally," and it may be that "every society is committed to retribution tied to proportionality but utilizes its own scale."[24] She observes that the *lex talionis* (the law of retaliation, exemplified by "an eye for an eye, a tooth for a tooth") is widespread among tribal societies and among the major religions of the world. Her main point is that retribution, "both in the form of *lex talionis*—strict proportionality—and in the form of blood money or compensation—general proportionality—existed in ancient civilization,"[25] and she cites the distinguished legal scholar David Daube, who makes a much more ambitious claim: that "[t]he two notions are so frequent, they appear in sources so different in all other respects, they underlie terms so ancient . . . and, it may be added, they are of so universal a nature, occurring in the ancient and modern literatures of all nations, that we must assume their existence right from the beginnings of any social life."[26]

She accounts for the practice of the feud in this light as depending on "the failure to satisfy *lex talionis*," and thus involving a commitment to the principle of it, and as "a carefully controlled mechanism" among peoples lacking a centralized political authority.[27] Of course, from a Western perspective, collective responsibility "does violate the idea of punishing only the person who committed the act in question," but it can be viewed as providing "an immensely powerful deterrent to violence."[28] In general, she argues that one "of the most important features of retribution . . . is to function as a limit to violence," that it is "an effective machinery for restoring social cohesion," and that it expresses "respect for human life," since the group has the duty to avenge the death of one of its members.[29] It seems, in short, that "most peoples in the world reject arbitrary, indiscriminate killing" and that all cultures have mechanisms that are intended to limit violence and to prevent needless killing.[30] (Indeed, Renteln cites Westermarck to make the Montaigne-like point that it is modern societies that are, in this respect, the true barbarians.) In conclusion she asks whether the fact that "cultures are committed to limits on arbitrary killing and violence" has "practical implications for universal human rights standards." She recognizes that this "will not resolve the arguments about infanticide and abortion, for some societies view these acts as arbitrary, unjustified killings while others will take the opposite view."[31] But she suggests that if "societies were to vote according to their own ideals," they would have to condemn "the arbitrary deprivation of life that is genocide" and that the fact in question "may provide a foundation for human rights, in particular those against torture and arbitrary killing."[32]

It is an intriguing suggestion, but what is especially telling, in relation to the Habermas-Scanlon positions discussed above, is that Renteln's evidence appears to be evidence of widespread, possibly universal condemnation of *arbitrariness*—that is, *lack of justification*. Of course, what counts as justified varies cross-culturally, but not, one presumes, indefinitely, and the limits of that variation look like a highly significant topic for empirical research.

The second way in which ethnography bears on the

Habermassian ideal of democratic discourse is simply by following through the implications of relevant field-work. Consider the much-discussed issue of clitoridec-tomy. In a subtle article entitled "Searching for 'Voices': Feminism, Anthropology, and the Global Debate over Female Genital Operations," Christine Walley shows how the "best interests" of the women involved can be contradictory.[33] Her fieldwork was in western Kenya, where, she reports, there was a great deal of public sup-port by young people for initiation. "For them to criti-cize circumcision publicly or to reject it," she writes, "would have led to accusations of cowardice, to social ostracism, and perhaps to physical violence,"[34] as one of them acknowledged had happened in the past. After witnessing an initiation ceremony at which circumci-sion took place, Walley invited four young women back to her house. They began by assuring her that the cus-tom was good. One of them, "who had recently been initiated and who had a look of religious ecstasy on her face that startled me, argued that it was something a person had to accept with her 'whole being' and when one did so, one did not feel the pain." Would they, Wal-ley asked, regret the ceremony later? To this they replied "in a light but serious tone, 'But we are already regret-ting it!,'" thereby revealing that "there was no delusion among these adolescent girls . . . about how it would af-fect their sexual pleasure. I asked whether they wanted their daughters to be 'circumcised.' One said she would because it was an important custom to continue; a second, after some thought, said she would not; and Mary, whose initiation photos we were perusing, looked uncom-fortable and declined to comment."[35] Walley notes that these interactions were "complex and full of nuances."[36] They give some hint of where "practical discourses" that test the justifiability of practices can lead, for they begin to open up crucial questions about voluntariness, acquiescence, and domination, and the range of feasible choices available to those involved.[37]

Not everyone, however, is persuaded that finding a universalistic basis for norms of morality in the narrow sense is an admirable project. Perhaps this very conception of morality is culturally specific to the West? Bernard Williams focuses on morality in this narrow sense but, while recognizing that it is part of the outlook of "almost all of us," views it as a "peculiar institution" and thinks "we would be better off without it."[38] He sees it as "a particular development of the ethical, one that has a special significance in modern Western culture. It peculiarly emphasizes certain ethical notions rather than others, developing in particular a special notion of obligation, and it has some peculiar presuppositions. In view of these features, it is also, I believe, something we should treat with a special skepticism."[39] Williams's complaint is that morality in its narrowness offers an impoverished view of the ethical life and, in particular, tries "to make everything into obligations," seen as stringent and attracting blame when broken and encouraging the idea that "only an obligation can beat an obligation."[40] But this is to mistake the proper role of narrow and universally applicable moral norms, that is, to serve as a threshold or filter or hurdle (choose your metaphor). The role of narrow morality is to provide a set of "side-constraints" on our valued activities and practices. It is to pose a *test* that ways of life—embodying values and norm-governed practices—must pass to be acceptable: the test of being justifiable to all involved in and affected by them. If your way of life fails the test, it violates the minimal standards of the universal core of morality.

Sometimes there can be a direct conflict between what core morality requires and what a particular moral code requires of its adherents. Take, for instance, honor killings or the honor code of the American South. Family honor is certainly a value that counts as moral in the broad sense, and we counted the norms of the "culture of honor" of the American South as moral in Chapter 3. And yet killing a sister or a cousin who has been "compromised" according to the code (for instance, by being raped) or resorting readily to violence to protect the reputation of oneself or one's group will never pass a universal justifiability test. Defending your honor bears many of the marks of being moral in the broad sense. The honor code is a matter of high importance. It concerns what is taken to be the well-being of others or the community. It is not, on the face of it, self-interested or egocentric. To succeed is to exhibit virtue, and failure or neglect will bring with it guilt and shame and punishment by others. And it invokes stringent obligations. Yet its (direct and indirect) victims have every reason to reject it.

Universal Values

I suggested above that, in distinguishing the moral from the ethical, we view morality as applying anywhere and everywhere and directing attention to the duties or obligations I have to other human beings viewed, from the standpoint of justice, as possessors of rights. The ethical, by contrast, refers to the values and ideals that inhere in one or another specific way of life—and these will, of course, be multiple and sometimes, as we have seen, mutually incompatible. But now a further question arises. Values are subjective (and intersubjective). They indicate how people view their choices and their lives—their conceptions of what can make these good rather than bad, what they count as important or worthwhile. But can values also be *objective*? Can one identify components of well-being that are present within any life that goes well rather than badly: conditions of human flourishing? The question comes from Aristotle and, though she does not give Aristotle's answer, it has been addressed in the writings of Martha Nussbaum.

Together with the economist Amartya Sen, Nussbaum has developed what they have both called "the capabilities approach." Sen's interest is in how to compare and even measure "the quality of life"; Nussbaum's is in finding principles to provide constitutional guarantees and guide law and public policy. Both were dissatisfied with standard economic approaches to questions of justice that focused either on the distribution of resources or on utility, or preference satisfaction. They were also impelled to go beyond John Rawls's theory of justice, which also focuses on resources and thus fails to consider that individuals differ in their needs for resources and in their capacities to convert resources into valued ways of living, or what Nussbaum and Sen call "functioning." For instance, "women who begin from a position of traditional deprivation and powerlessness will frequently require special attention and aid to arrive at a level of capability that the more powerful can easily attain."[41] What really matters, after all, is how people are actually enabled to live their lives: what they are actually able to do and be.

Nussbaum's key idea is that there is a range of distinctively human abilities that "exert a moral claim that they should be developed." Of course, not all human abilities exert such a claim (for example, the capacity for cruelty): only those that "have been evaluated as valuable from an ethical viewpoint."[42] There is thus a set of "core human entitlements that should be respected and implemented by the governments of all nations, as a bare minimum of what respect for human dignity requires."[43] As in the discussion earlier of moral norms, Nussbaum also employs the metaphor of a *threshold*, but here it marks the level of each capability beneath which "truly human functioning is not available to citizens[44]; the social goal is to get all above it (the phrase "truly human," she notices, comes from the early Marx, who wrote of the human being as a being "in need of a totality of human life activities").

She has developed a list of broadly defined "central human capabilities," refining and revising it over the years—a list that derives from extensive cross-cultural discussion and what she claims to be "an intuitively powerful idea of truly human functioning that has roots in many different traditions and is independent of any particular metaphysical or religious view."[45] It gives, she claims, "an account of minimum core social entitlements, and it is compatible with different views about how to handle issues of justice and distribution that would arise once all citizens are above the threshold level."[46] The latest version of the list identifies ten central human capabilities under these headings: life; bodily health; bodily integrity; senses, imagination, and thought; emotions; practical reason; affiliation; other species; play; and control over one's environment. The assumption is that all individuals, provided with the right educational and material support, can become fully capable of all of them and that the state's role is to do what can be done to remedy unequal starting points due to natural endowments, luck, and power. In general, the state must enable people to function in all these ways, leaving them free to determine their own course: those with plenty of food can, after all, choose to fast; those with normal opportunities for sexual satisfaction can choose to be celibate. Moreover, these ways of functioning are irreducibly *plural*: we cannot "satisfy the need for one of them by giving a larger amount of another one." There is a limit to the extent to which they can be subjected to trade-offs or quantitative cost-benefit analysis: there is "a tragic aspect to any choice in which citizens are pushed below the threshold in any one of the central areas."[47] (This is the case, for instance, when political liberty is sacrificed for economic growth.)

"In Defense of Universal Values" is the title of a chapter in which one version of this list appears,[48] and Nussbaum elsewhere stresses that her approach is "fully universal: the capabilities in question are held to be important for each and every citizen, in each and every nation, and each person is to be treated as an end. The approach is in this way similar to the international human rights approach; indeed, I view the capabilities approach as one species of a human rights approach. Arguing in favor of a set of cross-cultural norms and against the positions of cultural relativists has been an important dimension of the approach."[49]

Does Nussbaum's approach succeed in defending a set of universal values? More precisely, that defense raises two questions. First, does she succeed in showing that the ten centrally important capabilities are "held to be important"—that is, that they are *values*—"for each and every citizen in each and every nation"? And second, does she succeed in showing that, if this is so, she has arrived at an objective account of at least some of the conditions of human flourishing: that these *subjective* values are *objective,* and that we are therefore entitled to judge their remediable absence as a failure to respect human dignity, a failure to treat each person as an end and thus as "truly human"?

Nussbaum justifies her list of ten capabilities as "central requirements of a life with dignity."[50] They are, however, she admits, "specified in a somewhat abstract and general way."[51] Part of the idea of the list is its "*multiple realizability*: its members can be more concretely specified in accordance with local beliefs and circumstances. It is thus designed to leave room for a reasonable pluralism in specification. The threshold level of each of the central capabilities will need more precise determination, as citizens work towards a consensus for political purposes."[52] The point of the list is to provide guidance for constitution-makers and for law and public policy, so one must leave "room for the activities of specifying and deliberating by citizens and their legislatures and courts."[53] So, she suggests, Germany and the United States, given their different histories, can regulate free speech and political organizing differently, whereas "it seems plausible for governments to ban female genital mutilation, even when practiced by adults without coercion: for, in addition to long term health risks, the practice involves the permanent removal of the capability for most sexual pleasure, although individuals should of course be free to choose not to have sexual pleasure if they prefer not to."[54]

The difficulty here is to see what role to assign to "local beliefs and circumstances" in deciding where the limits lie to interpretations of the "abstract and general" central capabilities. Where the prevailing local view is to see cliteridectomy as part of a life with dignity and as essential to the capability of "affiliation," how is the matter to be decided? Nussbaum's answer is to say that this is up to citizens and their legislatures and courts, but her theory seems to offer no more than confidence that they will share her view of what seems plausible.

Let us, however, assume (and it is a large assumption) that this difficulty can be overcome and turn to the second question raised above. Does she succeed in showing that the shared subjective values are objective? Does recognizing the assumed fact that the central capabilities are, at some level, universally valued entitle us to judge their remediable absence as a failure to respect human dignity, a failure to treat each person as an end and thus as "truly human"? Here there looms a second troubling difficulty raised by her capabilities approach. Is this not a perfect mirror image of the non sequitur committed by the moral relativist that I identified at the beginning of this chapter—the move from observing the diversity of morals to concluding that *therefore* there is no one true morality and no privileged value perspective? As an observer, you note, with Nussbaum, that "we can arrive at an enumeration of central elements of truly human functioning that can command a broad cross-cultural consensus"[55] and that there is an idea of human dignity that has "broad cross-cultural resonance and intuitive power," which views the human being as "a dignified free being who shapes his or her own life in cooperation and reciprocity with others, rather than being passively shaped or pushed around by the world in the manner of a 'flock' or 'herd' animal."[56] (You further note that, unlike the language of rights, the language of capabilities is "not strongly linked to one particular cultural and historical tradition, as the language of rights is believed to be."[57] In fact, the idea of rights has deep roots in many traditions, but talk of capabilities enables us to bypass that debate.) You then conclude—you are now a person with moral views making moral judgments—that *therefore* you have attained, if not "an exhaustive account of what is worthwhile in life," at least a partial such account. Is this *therefore* any less misleading than the *therefore* that led from the observation of factual moral diversity to relativist conclusions?

The only path out of this difficulty that I can see is the path that Nussbaum herself takes. This is to claim that the central capabilities are universally evaluated as valuable from an ethical standpoint and that this observation does not entail but is, rather, compelling *evidence* for her normative ethical theory of truly human functioning.[58] Her idea is that there is (to use once more John Rawls's helpful phrase) "an *overlapping consensus* on the part of people with otherwise very different views of human life,"[59] as indicated, for instance, by literatures across the world. Tragic literature, in particular, suggests that there is a shared sense of waste and loss when a human being is "given a life that blights powers of human action and expression,"[60] a sense that crosses cultural boundaries. Such evidence can be seen as supporting (though it does not entail) her ethical standpoint; it refutes the suggestion that it is arbitrary and, in particular, that it is biased toward liberal individualism (though aspects of it doubtless still are). That standpoint is interesting and distinctive in that it combines value pluralism—the capabilities are not to be traded off against one another—and universalism. And it is worth noting that Berlin, with whose account of value pluralism we began Chapter 4, came in the end to a similar view, commenting that one "can exaggerate the absence of common ground. A great many people believe, roughly speaking, the same sort of thing. More people in more countries at more times accept more common values than is often believed."[61] In his last essay he wrote that "[a]ll human beings must have some common values or they cease to be human," adding that he was a pluralist, not a relativist, because those values are objective, "part of the essence of humanity rather than arbitrary creations of men's subjective fancies."[62]

Conclusion

Moral relativism disturbs and attracts, and it disturbs because it attracts. That is because, unlike relativism about factual knowledge and science, it can affect how we live our lives. Its message is not, as its advocates typically say, *tolerance* but rather *abstention*—denial of "our" right to judge the beliefs and practices of others, which goes together with the corollary they seldom mention: denial of "their" right to judge "ours." It results from a switch of perspectives. From your observation of the ever more vivid diversity of and conflicts between modes of thought and ways of life across the globe and in its cities, you conclude, as someone with moral views and making moral judgments, that confidence in their objectivity and universal applicability is misplaced: they are merely local and have no authority beyond the ambit of yourself and your fellows. Moral judgments, in short, always require a relativizing clause. The observation of diversity and conflict is hardly new; it goes back to the ancient Greeks and became commonplace from the Age of Discoveries, but the conclusion is modern. In Chapter 2 I sketched its first stirrings in Montaigne and its doctrinal development by the cultural relativist anthropologists. This raised the key issue of where moral authority comes from and thus the respective roles of reason, custom, and nature. In explaining our making of moral judgments, what part is played by rational reflection, what part by the internalization of norms and values, and what part by innate instincts or capacities? To what extent are our moral views and judgments mere *rationalizations* of what our socialization, evolutionary history, and innate equipment combine to deliver in different settings? Such questions are under intense investigation among moral psychologists and cognitive scientists today.

To what extent is the claim that the world contains multiple conflicting moralities true? *Do* we observe this or do we only think we do? In Chapters 3 and 4 we have considered this question, which turns out to be more difficult to answer than is often thought, partly because of conceptual imprecision, partly because of a lack of systematically acquired evidence, and partly because of the difficulties of interpreting it. But despite these difficulties, we concluded that there may be grounds for thinking that there is a diversity of moral norms (in the broad sense of "moral") and that the so-called fact of value pluralism is indeed a fact, though not one that links different values to distinct cultures viewed as bounded and integrated wholes.

Recognizing this, however, provides no reason for switching perspectives and committing the non sequitur of embracing moral relativism. Indeed, as I suggested, no one made that move until modern times. What motivates those inclined to make it today is the sense that we live in a postmetaphysical and foundationless world. Those who lack that sense are not so inclined and so roundly condemn moral relativism. Those who have it may be in search of arguments for the universal applicability of moral and ethical judgments, and I have suggested two such lines of argument—ways of reasoning—deriving respectively from Kant and from Aristotle.

There is, however, a set of further considerations that motivate people who are inclined to take the moral relativist turn. I began the Preface to this book by juxtaposing two widely shared intuitions that appear to be in direct conflict with one another. One is the thought that there are actions and modes of behavior that are right and others that are wrong universally; and that people everywhere are harmed if they are mistreated in certain ways or lack access to certain basic goods, services, and opportunities. The other intuition is the thought that is captured by the question Who are we to judge other cultures? Who are we, we may ask, to apply our standards to the adherents of other moral and religious systems? And I suggested that the second intuition, when developed, leads to moral relativism.

These two intuitions now stand in need of some refinement and commentary. The first, universalist intuition is these days somewhat narrower in focus, especially when framed in the discourse of human rights. Within that framework, we focus on actions that are universally wrong rather than those that are universally right. The latter concern seems moralistic rather than moral; we *proscribe,* say, torture and rape but we are reluctant to *prescribe* how people ought to act and live their lives. The idea of human rights suggests an area within which actions and activities within a certain range are to be prohibited anywhere and everywhere and, if performed, punished; and a set of entitlements that every human being on the planet is assumed to have. The second intuition raises the question of our entitlement to judge, and in particular to condemn, the beliefs and practices of others. But notice that the raising of that question results from the perception that those others resent our judgments and the thought that they have good grounds for that resentment.

There is, of course, a long history that warrants taking that resentment seriously and viewing it as often justified. Cultural imperialism, Eurocentrism, orientalism, ethnocentrism, and sometimes straightforward racism were inseparable from the imperialist era—from its political rhetoric and popular attitudes and from its literature and social science, not least its anthropology. Sensitivity to all this has developed, since the end of colonialism, to the point where, as Robert Frost quipped, "a liberal is a man too broad-minded to take his own side in a quarrel." This situation provides fertile ground for moral relativism. The very idea of universalism in ethics and political thought is sometime criticized as inherently ethnocentric,[63] and so the project of establishing and transplanting human rights across the globe comes to seem like a further case of Western, or rather Northern, ideological hegemony.

In her fine study *Human Rights and Gender Violence: Translating International Law into Local Justice*,[64] the anthropologist Sally Merry comments on the parallels and, indeed, continuities here. As with colonial legal transplants, human rights law is "dedicated to transforming family structure, land and labor relations and the tie between the individual and the state."[65] Moreover the proponents of human rights are the very same colonial powers, and their targets are the ex-colonies. Often the old imperialist habits of contrasting more with less advanced societies, civilization with barbarism, creep back into the debates, and the move to human rights establishes "the terrain of social justice as the law and the state, not religion or community. At the same time it imports through the back door assumptions about oppositions between rights and culture that were fundamental during imperialism and are still embedded in human rights rhetoric."[66] And finally, the "human rights system is deeply shaped by power and resource inequalities between the global North and the global South, as was the imperial system."[67] This determines the flow of funding, the recognition of NGOs (non-governmental organizations), and the selection

of projects, avoiding structural changes that would re-
duce global inequality and capitalist expansion.

And yet the differences are decisive. The generation of
human rights laws, declarations, and other documents is
a global process of transnational consensus building. As
such it is highly imperfect, in the ways indicated and others, but it incorporates the very standards by which it can
be criticized and improved. Moreover it is, as Merry observes, "being appropriated around the globe by national
and local actors who see the potential benefits of a human rights framework and redefine their agendas in
these terms" and offers "a new cultural framework that
breaks with past ways of understanding behavior."[68] Such
a break, she writes, "is critical in changing behavior such
as wife battering that was long accepted as normal but
must be redefined as offensive in order to diminish its
frequency. This is a process of appropriation rather than
imposition."[69] What is at issue here is "the boundary between acceptable forms of violence against women, defined as discipline, and unacceptable forms, defined as
abuse." Indeed,

> [r]edrawing this boundary is at the heart of the human
> rights project concerning violence against women.
> Activists seek to redefine violence from discipline to
> abuse. In order to shift the boundary of appropriate
> violence, activists need to alter such fundamental
> institutions as marriage. Their opponents claim that
> this form of discipline is essential to the preservation
> of marriage. Many religious and political leaders resist
> making the changes that are required to improve
> women's safety, often invoking the need to protect

culture. Arguments about preserving culture become the basis for defending male control over women.[70]

In short, the question Who are we to judge other cultures? is a bad question. The judgment challenging patriarchal attitudes and practices is local and also global, in part the outcome of global processes rendered into the vernacular, and it is the patriarchs, not their local critics, who are preoccupied with "culture."

What then remains of the case for moral relativism? I have argued that it embodies a non sequitur: that acknowledging the facts of moral diversity and value pluralism does not entail abstention from judging others (and their judging us). I then suggested various motives that lead people to draw this conclusion anyway. The road to moral relativism is paved with plausible contentions, and I suggested that these are less plausible and more contentious than they seem. The loss of a widely shared worldview with secure metaphysical and religious foundations (was it really so consensual and secure?) does not render us unable to make universally applicable judgments. The idea that radically diverse values inhere in "cultures," like so many windowless boxes viewed in holistic and essentialist terms, cannot be sustained. The postcolonial and multicultural contexts of our time do not require us to see the discourse and practice of human rights as ethnocentric and ideological.

Yet I doubt that many readers will be persuaded that, because of these arguments, moral relativism has now lost all its appeal. This largely comes from its *recognition* of the variety of human ways of living and the sheer improbability that we just happen to have found the best way, the one true morality. That we have is what is suggested by the only apparent alternative view, namely moral absolutism. Even liberals can take this position. Thus Brian Barry, in the course of a fine defense of liberal principles and attack on abuses of the notion of "culture," can write that "precisely because human beings are virtually identical as they come from the hand of nature—at any rate at the level of groups—there is nothing straightforwardly absurd about the idea that there is a single best way for human beings to live, allowing whatever adjustments are necessary for different physical environments."[71]

There may be nothing "straightforwardly absurd" about this idea, but there is nothing remotely convincing about it either. Which suggests that the surviving appeal of moral relativism is indeed that it recognizes the idea that there is no single best way for human beings to live; or, to express the same idea in another way, that there are many such best ways, where what is best is internal to a range of alternative conceptions of the good.

How are we to acknowledge the truth of this last idea while retaining our capacity to make moral judgments? The problem with moral relativism as we have discussed it throughout this book is that it debunks the authority of moral standards, claiming that it derives from social norms or conventions; and that it denies the reality of moral disagreements. Suppose that two people—a human-rights activist and a wife-beating husband—are in disagreement over the question of whether wife-beating is abusive or a necessary defense of marriage. The moral relativist has only two ways of judging this situation. One is to say that the husband's view is the right one, since what is right and wrong is decided by the prevailing norms of the local culture (this is the cultural relativist view; as Ruth Benedict remarked: "Morality . . . is a convenient term for socially approved habits"). Alternatively, given that each appeals to a different set of norms and values, the relativist will declare the disagreement to be only apparent, since each is right relative to each one's norms and values.

Acknowledging the surviving truth in moral relativism—that there are multiple best ways for human beings to live—can be combined with making moral judgments and thus recognizing the authority of moral standards and the reality of moral disagreements. As suggested above, one can take the Kantian line of asking whether a given practice can be justified to all those affected, or one can take the Aristotelian line of asking whether it drags those involved in it below the threshold of one or more of the central human capabilities. Many ways of life—involving different forms of marriage and gender relations, for example[72] —may pass these tests, but wife-battering certainly will not.

NOTES

1. Relativism: Cognitive and Moral

1. Friedrich Nietzsche, *On the Genealogy of Morality*, ed. Keith Ansell-Pierson, trans. Carol Diethe (Cambridge: Cambridge University Press, 1994), 92.
2. BBC News Magazine: 20 April 2005 (http://news.bbc .co.uk/1/hi/magazine/4460673.stm).
3. Allan Bloom, *The Closing of the American Mind: How Higher Education Has Failed Democracy and Impoverished the Souls of Today's Students* (New York: Simon and Schuster, 1987), 34.
4. Nietzsche, *Genealogy of Morality*, 92.
5. Bernard Williams, "The End of Explanation" (a review of Thomas Nagel's *The Last Word*), *New York Review of Books* 45, no. 18 (1998), 40–41.
6. Marcy Darnovsky, "Overhauling the Meaning Machine: An Interview with Dona Haraway," *Socialist Review* 21, no. 2 (1991), 66.
7. Both quotations come from Paul Boghossian, *Fear of Knowledge: Against Relativism and Constructivism* (Oxford: Clarendon Press, 2006), 2.
8. Renato Rosaldo, *Culture and Truth: The Remaking of Social Analysis* (Boston: Beacon Press, 1989), 21.
9. Paul Feyerabend, *Against Method: Outline of an Anarchistic Theory of Knowledge* (London: NLB, 1975), 295.
10. Thomas Kuhn, *The Structure of Scientific Revolutions*, 3rd ed. (Chicago: Chicago University Press, 1996). First published in 1962.
11. Bruno Latour, *Science in Action: How to Follow Scientists and Engineers Through Society* (Cambridge, MA: Harvard University Press, 1985), 258.
12. Paul Feyerabend, "Atoms and Consciousness," *Common Knowledge* 1, no. 1 (1992), 28–32; Bruno Latour, "Why Has Critique Run Out of Steam? From Matters of Fact to Matters of Concern," *Critical Inquiry* 30, no. 2 (2004), 225–48.

13. Ian Hacking, *The Social Construction of What?* (Cambridge, MA: Harvard University Press, 1999).

14. Karl Mannheim, *Ideology and Utopia: An Introduction to the Sociology of Knowledge* (London: Routledge and Kegan Paul, 1936; paperback edition 1960), 237. Citation is to the latter edition.

15. Robert K. Merton, *Social Theory and Social Structure,* rev. ed. (Glencoe, IL: Free Press, 1957), 507.

16. Benjamin Lee Whorf, *Language, Thought and Reality* (Boston: MIT Press; New York: Wiley, 1954), 213.

17. Edward Sapir, "The Status of Linguistics as a Science," *Language* 5, no. 4 (1929), 209.

18. Lucien Lévy-Bruhl, *Les functions mentales dans les sociétés inférieures* (Paris: Alcan, 1910), 30–31.

19. E. E. Evans-Pritchard, *Witchcraft, Oracles and Magic among the Azande* (Oxford: Clarendon Press, 1937).

20. Peter Winch, "Understanding a Primitive Society," *American Philosophical Quarterly* 1, no. 4 (1964), 307–24, reprinted in *Rationality,* ed. Bryan R. Wilson (Oxford: Blackwell, 1970).

21. Ludwig Wittgenstein, *On Certainty,* eds. G. E. M. Anscombe and G. H. von Wright, trans. Denis Paul and G. E. M. Anscombe (Oxford: Blackwell, 1975), paras 609, 612.

22. Ludwig Wittgenstein, *Philosophical Investigations,* trans. G. E. M. Anscombe (Oxford: Blackwell, 1953), para 217.

23. Gananath Obeyesekere, *The Apotheosis of Captain Cook: European Mythmaking in the Pacific* (Princeton: Princeton University Press, 1992). New edition with afterword by the author, 1997, 16–17, 19.

24. Marshall Sahlins, *How "Natives" Think: About Captain Cook, for Example* (Chicago: Chicago University Press, 1995), 9, 155, 158, 14.

25. Richard Rorty, "Does Academic Freedom Have Philosophical Presuppositions? Academic Freedom and the Future of the University," *Academe* 80, no. 6 (1994), 57.

26. Richard Rorty, *Philosophy and the Mirror of Nature* (Princeton: Princeton University Press, 1981), 328–29.

27. Thomas Kuhn, *The Structure of Scientific Revolutions,* 2nd ed. (Chicago: Chicago University Press, 1970), 148.

28. Ibid., 150.

29. Ibid., 150–51, 153.

30. Barry Barnes and David Bloor, "Relativism, Rationalism and the Sociology of Knowledge," in *Rationality and Relativism,* eds. Martin Hollis and Steven Lukes (Oxford: Blackwell, 1982), 22.

31. Ibid., 22–23.

32. Steven Shapin and Simon Schaffer, *Leviathan and the Air Pump* (Princeton: Princeton University Press, 1985), 283, 344.

33. Barnes and Bloor, "Relativism, Rationalism," 45.

34. Latour, "Why Has Critique Run Out of Steam?" 225.

35. For recent examples, see Thomas Nagel, *The Last Word* (Oxford: Oxford University Press, 1997); Simon Blackburn, *Truth: A Guide for the Perplexed* (London: Penguin, 2005); and Paul Boghossian, *Fear of Knowledge: Against Relativism and Constructivism* (Oxford: Clarendon Press, 2006).

36. Ernest Gellner, *Postmodernism, Reason and Religion* (London and New York: Routledge, 1992), 50.

37. Gellner, *Postmodernism, Reason and Religion,* 54.

38. Bernard Williams, *Ethics and the Limits of Philosophy* (London: Fontana, 1985), 136.

39. T. M. Scanlon, *What We Owe to Each Other* (Cambridge, MA: Harvard University Press, Belknap Press, 1998), 331.

40. Williams, *Ethics,* 160–61.

41. Bernard Williams, "Human Rights and Relativism," in *In the Beginning Was the Deed: Realism and Moralism in Political Argument,* ed. Geoffrey Hawthorn (Princeton and Oxford: Princeton University Press, 2005), 66.

42. Williams, *Ethics,* 163.

43. Williams, "Human Rights," 68–69.
44. Mary Douglas, *How Institutions Think* (Syracuse, NY: Syracuse University Press, 1986), 113.
45. Clifford Geertz, "Anti Anti-Relativism," *American Anthropologist* 86, no. 2 (1984), 263–78, reprinted in Geertz, *Available Light: Anthropological Reflections on Philosophical Topics* (Princeton: Princeton University Press, 2000), 65.
46. Claude Lévi-Strauss, *Structural Anthropology,* vol. 2, trans. Monique Layton (New York: Basic Books, 1976), 340.
47. Edward Westermarck, *Ethical Relativity* (New York: Harcourt Brace, 1932), 61, 289.
48. Richard Brandt, *Ethical Theory: The Problems of Normative and Critical Ethics* (Englewood Cliffs, NJ: Prentice-Hall, 1959), 284.
49. J. L. Mackie, *Ethics: Inventing Right and Wrong* (Harmondsworth, UK: Penguin, 1977), 48–49.
50. Douglas, *How Institutions Think,* 118.
51. Brian Barry, "Circumstances of Justice and Future Generations," in *Obligations to Future Generations,* eds. R. I. Sikora and B. Barry (Philadelphia: Temple University Press, 1978), 22.
52. Douglas, *How Institutions Think,* 119, 117.
53. M. Smith, *The Moral Problem* (Oxford: Blackwell, 1994), 9.
54. J. W. Cook, *Morality and Cultural Differences* (New York and Oxford: Oxford University Press, 1999), 17.
55. William Graham Sumner, *Folkways* (Boston: Ginn, 1934), Sec. 439. Mentor Books edition, New York, 1960, 355.
56. Ruth Benedict, "Anthropology and the Abnormal," *Journal of General Psychology* 101 (1934), 73, reprinted in *Personal Character and Cultural Milieu,* ed. Douglas Haring (Syracuse, NY: Syracuse University Press, 1956).

2. Reason, Custom, and Nature

1. Michel de Montaigne, *The Complete Essays*, trans. M. A. Screech (London: Penguin, 1981), 130.
2. Herodotus, *The Histories*, ed. and trans. A. D. Godley (Cambridge, MA: Harvard University Press, 1920), Book 3, Chapter 38, Sec. 3, 1. The quotation from an otherwise unknown poem by Pindar appears in Plato's *Gorgias*.
3. Mary Midgley, *Can't We Make Moral Judgments?* (New York: St. Martin's Press, 1991), 84.
4. Montaigne, *Complete Essays*, 130, 125.
5. Ibid., 126.
6. Ibid., 130.
7. Tzvetan Todorov, *On Human Diversity: Nationalism, Racism and Exoticism in French Thought*, trans. Catherine Porter (Cambridge, MA: Harvard University Press, 1993), 34.
8. Montaigne, *Complete Essays*, 132.
9. Ibid., 133.
10. Ibid., 235–36.
11. Ibid., 236.
12. Ibid., 234.
13. Ibid., 236–40.
14. Ibid., 231.
15. Todorov, *On Human Diversity*, 42.
16. J. W. Cook, *Morality and Cultural Differences* (New York and Oxford: Oxford University Press, 1999), 66.
17. Montaigne, *Complete Essays*, 1084.
18. Ibid., 1101.
19. See Isaiah Berlin, *Vico and Herder: Two Studies in the History of Ideas* (New York: Viking, 1976).
20. Michele M. Moody-Adams, *Fieldwork in Familiar Places: Morality, Culture, and Philosophy* (Cambridge, MA: Harvard University Press, 1997), 21.
21. Melville Herskovits, "Some Further Comments on Cultural Relativism," *American Anthropologist* 60 (April 1958), 270.
22. Clyde Kluckholm, *Mirror for Man* (New York and Toronto: McGraw-Hill, 1949), 26.

23. Elvin Hatch, *Culture and Morality: The Relativity of Values in Anthropology* (New York: Columbia University Press, 1983), 53–54.

24. Ruth Benedict, *Patterns of Culture* (London: George Routledge, 1935), 17.

25. Robert Redfield, *Human Nature and the Study of Society: The Papers of Robert Redfield*, ed. Margaret P. Redfield (Chicago: Chicago University Press, 1962), 458–59.

26. Ibid.

27. Benedict, *Patterns of Culture*, 201.

28. Melville Herskovits, *Man and His Works* (New York: Knopf, 1960), 76.

29. Philip Selznick, *The Moral Commonwealth* (Berkeley: University of California Press, 1992), 95.

30. Maurice Barrès, *Scènes et doctrines de nationlisme*, vol. 2 (Paris: Plon-Nourrit, 1922), 177.

31. Todorov, *On Human Diversity*, 60.

32. Elgin Williams, "Anthropology for the Common Man," *American Anthropologist*, n.s., 49, no. 1 (1947), 88.

33. Philip Selznick, *The Moral Commonwealth: Social Theory and the Promise of Community* (Berkeley: University of California Press, 1992), 113.

34. Robert Redfield, *The Primitive World and Its Transformation* (Ithaca, NY: 1953), 145.

35. Margaret Mead, *New Lives for Old* (New York: William Morrow, 1956), 442.

36. "Statement on Human Rights," *American Anthropologist*, n.s., 49, no. 3 (October–December 1947), 539, 543.

37. Marshall Sahlins, "Goodbye to Tristes Tropes: Ethnography in the Context of Modern World History," *Journal of Modern History* 65, no. 1 (1993), 3–4.

38. Carol Gilligan, *In a Different Voice* (Cambridge, MA: Harvard University Press, 1982).

39. Eliot Turiel, *The Development of Social Knowledge: Morality and Convention* (Cambridge: Cambridge University Press, 1983) and *The Culture of Morality: Social Development, Context and Conflict* (Cambridge: Cambridge University Press, 2002).

40. The first main critic of Turiel's distinction was Richard Shweder and his coauthors, who claimed (using evidence from both India and Chicago) that "the differentiation of moral events from conventional events is not necessarily a developmental universal and that the distinction between morality and convention, useful as it is within certain cultural world-views, may well be culture-specific." R. A. Shweder, M. Mahapatra, and J. G. Miller, "Culture and Moral Development," in *The Emergence of Morality in Young Children*, eds. Jerome Kagan and Sharon Lamb (Chicago: Chicago University Press, 1987), 72.

41. Daniel Kelly and others, "Harm, Affect and the Moral/Conventional Distinction," *Mind and Language* 22, no. 2 (2007), 117–31.

42. Jonathan Haidt, *The Happiness Hypothesis: Finding Modern Truth in Ancient Wisdom* (New York: Basic Books, 2006), 20 21, and "Sexual Morality: The Cultures and Reasons of Liberals and Conservatives," *Journal of Applied Social Psychology* 33 (2001), 191–221.

43. *Daedalus* (Fall 2004), 55–66.

44. *Psychological Review* 108, no. 4 (2001), 814–34.

45. Haidt, *Happiness Hypothesis*, 26, 21–22.

46. Joshua Greene, "The Secret Joke of Kant's Soul," in *Moral Pschology*, vol 3, *The Neuroscience of Morality: Emotion, Disease and Development*, ed. W. Sinnott-Armstrong (Cambridge: MIT Press, 2007), 43.

47. Ibid., 46.

48. Susan Dwyer, "How Good Is the Linguistic Analogy?" in *The Innate Mind*, vol. 2, *Culture and Cognition*, eds. Peter Carruthers, Stephen Laurence, and Stephen Stich (Oxford: Oxford University Press, 2007), 237–38.

49. J. Hernrich and others, "In Search of *Homo Economicus*: Behavioral Experiments in Fifteen Small-Scale Societies," *American Economic Review* 91, no. 2 (2001), 73–78.

50. Marc Hauser, *Moral Minds: How Nature Designed Our Universal Sense of Right and Wrong* (New York: HarperCollins, 2006), 422.

51. Dwyer, "How Good Is the Linguistic Analogy?" 247.
52. Hauser, *Moral Minds*, 230.
53. Ibid., 158–59.
54. See Emmanuel Dupoux and Pierre Jacob, "Universal Moral Grammar: A Critical Approach," *Trends in Cognitive Science* 11, no. 9 (2007), 373–78.

3. *The Diversity of Morals*

1. Morris Ginsberg, *On the Diversity of Morals* (London: Heinemann, 1956; Mercury Books, 1962), 100.
2. T. M. Scanlon, *What We Owe Each Other* (Cambridge, MA: Harvard University Press, Belknap Press, 1998), Chapter 4.
3. Jon Elster, *Explaining Social Behavior: More Nuts and Bolts for the Social Sciences* (Cambridge: Cambridge University Press, 2007), 104–7.
4. Marc Hauser, *Moral Minds: How Nature Designed Our Universal Sense of Right and Wrong* (New York: HarperCollins, 2006), 238.
5. Elster, *Explaining Social Behavior*, 364.
6. Susan Dwyer, "How Good Is the Linguistic Analogy?" in *The Innate Mind*, vol. 2, *Culture and Cognition*, eds. Peter Carruthers, Stephen Laurence, and Stephen Stich (Oxford: Oxford University Press, 2007), 240.
7. J. W. Cook, *Morality and Cultural Differences* (New York and Oxford: Oxford University Press, 1999), 82.
8. Richard A. Shweder, "What About Female Genital Mutilation?" and "Why Understanding Culture Matters in the First Place" in *Engaging Cultural Differences: The Multicultural Challenges in Liberal Democracies*, eds. R. Shweder, M. Minow, and H. Markus (New York: Russell Sage Foundation Press, 2002), 216–51.
9. Richard A. Shweder, *Thinking Through Cultures: Expeditions in Cultural Psychology* (Cambridge, MA: Harvard University Press, 1991), 17.
10. Ibid., 15.
11. Cook, *Morality and Cultural Differences*, 35–36.
12. Robert Redfield, *The Primitive World and Its Transfor-

mation (Ithaca, NY: Cornell University Press, 1953), 131–32.

13. Karl Duncker, "Ethical Relativity? (An Inquiry into the Psychology of Ethics)," *Mind* 48 (1939), 40–41.

14. K. J. Dover, *Greek Popular Morality: In the Time of Plato and Aristotle* (Indianapolis/Cambridge: Hackett, 1974), 273.

15. E. E. Evans-Pritchard, *Theories of Primitive Religion* (Oxford: Clarendon Press, 1965), 24, 43.

16. Cook, *Morality and Cultural Differences,* 70, 89.

17. Cited in ibid., 94.

18. Cited in ibid., 95.

19. Cited in ibid., 95–96.

20. Ruth Benedict, "Anthropology and the Abnormal," *Journal of General Psychology* 101 (1934), reprinted in *Personal Character and Cultural Milieu,* ed. Douglas Haring (Syracuse, NY: Syracuse University Press, 1956), 73. Citations are to the original article.

21. Ibid., 71.

22. Ibid., 67–68.

23. Cook, *Morality and Cultural Differences,* 97–101.

24. Benedict, "Anthropology and the Abnormal," 73.

25. Ibid.

26. Ibid., 78.

27. Ibid., 64.

28. Ibid., 72.

29. Ibid., 74.

30. Boas quoted in Cook, *Morality and Cultural Differences,* 66.

31. Ibid.

32. Franz Boas, "An Anthropologist's Credo," *Nation* 147 (1938), 202, cited in Cook, *Morality and Cultural Differences,* 74.

33. Cited by John Kekes, "Pluralism and the Value of Life," in *Cultural Pluralism and Moral Knowledge,* eds. Ellen Frankel Paul, Fred D. Miller Jr., and Jeffrey Paul (Cambridge: Cambridge University Press, 1994), 55.

34. Ibid.

35. Martha C. Nussbaum, *Women and Human Development: The Capabilities Approach* (Cambridge: Cambridge University Press, 2000), 192–93n43.

36. Colin Turnbull, *The Mountain People* (London: Picador, 1974).

37. Ibid., 210.

38. Ibid., 195.

39. Ibid., 180.

40. Ibid., 214.

41. Ibid., 151.

42. Ibid., 195.

43. Neil Levy, *Moral Relativism: A Short Introduction* (Oxford: Oneworld, 2002), 99.

44. Ibid.

45. Richard Brandt, "Ethical Relativism," in *The Encyclopedia of Philosophy,* ed. Paul Edwards, vol. 3 (New York: Macmillan, 1967), 75–78, reprinted in *Moral Relativism: A Reader,* eds. Paul K. Moser and Thomas L. Carson (New York: Oxford University Press, 2001), 26.

46. Ibid.

47. Michele M. Moody-Adams, *Fieldwork in Familiar Places: Morality, Culture, and Philosophy* (Cambridge, MA: Harvard University Press, 1997), 31.

48. Dan Sperber, "Apparently Irrational Beliefs," in *Rationality and Relativism,* eds. Martin Hollis and Steven Lukes (Oxford: Blackwell, 1982), 162.

49. Richard B. Brandt, *Ethical Theory: The Problems of Normative and Critical Ethics* (Englewood Cliffs, NJ: Prentice-Hall, 1959), 101–2.

50. Ibid., 102.

51. Richard B. Brandt, *Hopi Ethics* (Chicago: Chicago University Press, 1954), 245.

52. Ibid.

53. Ibid.

54. See Stefan Bargheer, "The Fools of the Leisure Class: Honor, Ridicule and the Emergence of Animal Protection Legislation in England, 1740–1840," *Archives européennes de sociologie* XLVII, no. 1 (2006), 3–35.

55. Kirkpatrick Sale, *The Conquest of Paradise* (New York: Knopf, 1990), 157.

56. Cited in Immanuel Wallerstein, *European Universalism: The Rhetoric of Power* (New York and London: New Press, 2006), 5. See also Bartolomé de Las Casas, *In Defense of the Indians,* ed. Stafford Poole (De Kalb: Northern Illinois University Press, 1992). For further discussion of Las Casas in this connection, see William J. Talbott, *Which Rights Should Be Universal?* (Oxford: Oxford University Press, 2005).

57. Condorcet, "*Sur l'Admission des femmes au droit de cité,*" in *Oeuvres,* eds. A. Condorcet-O'Connor and M. F. Arago, vol. 10 (Paris: Firmin-Didot, 1847), 121.

58. Brandt, *Ethical Theory,* 102.

59. Richard E. Nisbett and Dov Cohen, *Culture of Honor: The Psychology of Violence in the South* (Boulder, CO, and Oxford: Westview, 1996).

60. Ibid., 9.

61. Ibid., xvi.

62. Ibid., 4.

63. Ibid., 4–5.

64. Ibid., 10.

65. Ibid., 38.

66. Ibid.

67. See the critique by Philip Tetlock, reviewing the book in *Political Psychology* 20, no. 1 (1999), 211–13.

68. Nisbett and Cohen, *Culture of Honor,* 93.

69. Ibid.

70. John M. Doris and Stephen P. Stich, "As a Matter of Fact: Empirical Perspectives on Ethics," in *The Oxford Handbook of Contemporary Analytic Philosophy,* eds. F. Jackson and M. Smith (Oxford: Oxford University Press, 2003), 135.

71. Richard E. Nisbett, *The Geography of Thought: How Asians and Westerners Think Differently . . . and Why* (New York: Free Press, 2003).

72. Ibid., xx.

73. Ibid., 76–77.

74. Ibid., 77.
75. Ibid., 73.
76. Cited in Daniel A. Bell, *East Meets West: Human Rights and Democracy in East Asia* (Princeton: Princeton University Press, 2000), 96n121.
77. Moody-Adams, *Fieldwork in Familiar Places*, 36.
78. Ibid., 34.
79. Talbott, *Which Rights Should Be Universal?* 79, 78. Todorov treats Las Casas, by contrast, as a moral relativist in his *The Conquest of America*, trans. Richard Howard (New York: Harper and Row, 1984).
80. Ibid., 80.

4. Cultures and Values

1. Johann Gottfried Herder, *Ideen zur Philosophie der Geschichte der Menscheit,* Dritter Teil, Funfzehntes Buch (Deutsche Bibilothek in Berlin: 1914), 210.
2. Isaiah Berlin, "Alleged Relativism in Eighteenth-Century European Thought," in *The Crooked Timber of Humanity: Chapters in the History of Ideas* (London: John Murray, 1990), 79.
3. Isaiah Berlin, "Two Concepts of Liberty," in *Four Essays on Liberty* (London and Oxford: Oxford University Press, 1969), 167–72.
4. Max Weber, "Science as a Vocation," in *From Max Weber: Essays in Sociology,* trans. and eds. H. H. Gerth and C. Wright Mills (London: Routledge and Kegan Paul, 1948), 152, 143, 148.
5. Max Weber, "Politics as a Vocation," in *From Max Weber,* 123.
6. Isaiah Berlin, "The Originality of Machiavelli," in *Against the Current: Essays in the History of Ideas* (London: Hogarth Press, 1979), 69, 48, 50, 74.
7. Isiaiah Berlin, "John Stuart Mill and the Ends of Life," in *Four Essays,* 190.
8. Weber, 147, 148.
9. David Hume, "An Enquiry Concerning the Human Understanding," in *Enquiries Concerning the Human*

Understanding and Concerning the Principles of Morals, ed. L. A. Selby-Bigge, 2nd ed. (Oxford: Clarendon Press, 1902), Sec. VIII, Part 1, 83.

10. Michael Forster, trans. and ed., *Herder: Philosophical Writings* (New York: Cambridge University Press, 2002), 286.

11. J. G. Herder, *Outlines of a Philosophical History of Man*, trans. T. Churchill (New York: Bergman, 1966), 452.

12. F. M. Barnard, ed., *J. G. Herder on Social and Political Culture* (Cambridge: Cambridge University Press, 1969), 82.

13. Forster, *Herder*, 292.

14. Ibid., 186.

15. Ibid., 292.

16. Ibid., 423–24.

17. Johann Gottlieb Fichte, "Addresses to the German Nation: Thirteenth Address," in *The Political Thought of the German Romantics: 1793–1815*, ed. H. J. Reiss (Oxford: Blackwell, 1955), 108.

18. Jomo Kenyatta, *Facing Mount Kenya: The Tribal Life of the Gikuyu*, with introd. by B. Malinowski (New York: Vintage Books, 1965).

19. Ibid., 297.

20. Ibid., 304.

21. Ibid., 140.

22. Ibid., 129.

23. Ibid., 128.

24. Ibid., 130.

25. Ibid., xiii, x.

26. Seyla Benhabib, *The Claims of Culture: Equality and Diversity in the Global Era* (Princeton and Oxford: Princeton University Press, 2002), 3–4.

27. Will Kymlicka, *Multicultural Citizenship* (Oxford: Oxford University Press, 1995), 113.

28. Will Kymlicka, *Liberalism, Community and Culture* (Oxford; Clarendon Press, 1989), 165.

29. Paul M. Sniderman and Louk Hagendoorn, *When Ways of Life Collide: Multiculturalism and Its Discontents in*

the Netherlands (Princeton and Oxford: Princeton University Press, 2007).

30. Ibid., 129–30.

31. Ibid., 122.

32. Ibid., 135.

33. Samuel P. Huntington, *The Clash of Civilizations and the Remaking of World Order* (New York: Simon and Schuster, 1996).

34. Elaborated further in his subsequent book *Who Are We? The Challenge to America's Identity* (New York: Simon and Schuster, 2004).

35. Huntington, *Clash of Civilizations,* 306.

36. Ibid., 308.

37. Ibid., 306.

38. Ibid., 36.

39. Ibid., 28.

40. Ibid., 217.

41. Ibid., 238.

42. Cited in Joanne R. Bauer and Daniel A. Bell, eds., *The East Asian Challenge for Human Rights* (Cambridge: Cambridge University Press, 1999), 6.

43. See the excellent discussion of this in Alfred Stepan, *Arguing Comparative Politics* (Oxford: Oxford University Press, 2001), 229–32.

44. *Foreign Affairs* (November–December 1994), 189–94.

45. Joseph Chan, "A Confucian Perspective on Human Rights for Contemporary China," in Bauer and Bell, eds., *East Asian Challenge,* 212.

46. *The Analects of Confucius,* trans. Simon Leys (New York: W. W. Norton, 1997).

47. Salman Rushdie, "In Good Faith," in *Essays and Criticism, 1981–1991* (London: Granta; New York: Viking, 1991), 393, 394, 404.

48. Jeremy Waldron, "Minority Cultures and the Cosmopolitan Alternative," reprinted in *The Rights of Minority Cultures,* ed. Will Kymlicka (Oxford: Oxford University Press, 1995) Chapter 4, 95.

49. Ibid., 100.

50. Ibid., 100, 112.

51. James Clifford and George E. Markus, eds., *Writing Culture: The Poetics and Politics of Ethnography: A School of American Research Advanced Seminar* (Berkeley: University of California Press, 1986), 19.

52. Ibid., 16.

53. Jonathan Friedman, "Indigenous Struggles and the Discreet Charm of the Bourgeoisie," *Journal of World System Research* 5, no. 2 (1999), 409.

54. Ann Swidler, "Culture in Action: Symbols and Strategies," *American Sociological Review* 51 (April 1986), 273–86.

55. Ibid., 281, 273.

56. Ibid., 281.

57. Ibid., 277.

58. Ibid.

59. Ibid.

60. Ibid., 279.

61. Ibid., 282, 283.

62. Mary Midgley, *Can't We Make Moral Judgments?* (New York: St. Martin's Press, 1991), 90.

63. Claude Lévi-Strauss, *Race and History*, cited in Adam Kuper, *Culture: The Anthropologists' Account* (Cambridge, MA: Harvard University Press, 1999), 243.

64. Friedman, "Indigenous Struggles," 397.

65. Swidler, "Culture in Action," 277.

66. Joseph Raz, *Ethics in the Public Domain: Essays in the Morality of Law and Politics* (Oxford: Clarendon Press, 1994), 177.

67. See the discussion in Kwame Anthony Appiah, "The Trouble with Culture," in *The Ethics of Identity* (Princeton: Princeton University Press, 2004).

68. Kuper, *Culture*, 245–46.

69. Eric Wolf, *Europe and the People Without History* (Berkeley: University of California Press, 1982), 387.

70. Michele M. Moody-Adams, *Fieldwork in Familiar Places: Morality, Culture, and Philosophy* (Cambridge, MA: Harvard University Press, 1997), 53.

71. Sniderman and Hagendoorn, *When Ways of Life Collide*, 128–29.
72. But see Hans Joas, *The Genesis of Values,* trans. Gregory Moore (Cambridge: Polity, 2000) and Raymond Boudon, *The Origin of Values: Sociology and Philosophy of Beliefs* (New Brunswick and London: Transaction, 2001).
73. Jean-Paul Sartre, *Existentialism and Humanism*, trans. Philip Mairet (London: Methuen, 1948).

5. The Universal and the Relative

1. Raymond Boudon, *The Poverty of Relativism* (Oxford and Cambridge: Bardwell Press, 2004), 165.
2. Blaise Pascal, *Pensées,* Sec. 294.
3. Ibid., Secs. 599, 606.
4. Joseph Ratzinger, now Pope Benedict XVI, and Marcello Pera, *Without Roots: The West, Relativism, Christianity, Islam* (New York: Basic Books, 2006), 126, 134, 75.
5. Allan Bloom, *The Closing of the American Mind: How Higher Eduction Has Failed Democracy and Impoverished the Souls of Today's Students* (New York: Simon and Schuster, 1987), 380–81.
6. Kwame Anthony Appiah, *The Ethics of Identity* (Princeton: Princeton University Press, 2005), 252–53.
7. Michele M. Moody-Adams, *Fieldwork in Familiar Places: Morality, Culture, and Philosophy* (Cambridge, MA: Harvard University Press, 1997), 212.
8. Emile Durkheim, *Moral Education: A Study in the Theory and Application of the Sociology of Education,* trans. Everett K. Wilson and Herman Schnurer, ed. Everett K. Wilson (New York: Free Press of Glencoe, 1951), 45. See the discussion of Durkheim's view in Hans Joas, *The Genesis of Values,* trans. Gregory Moore (Cambridge: Polity, 2000), 66.
9. Durkheim, *Moral Education,* 45.
10. Ronald Dworkin, *Sovereign Virtue: The Theory and Practice of Equality* (Cambridge, MA: Harvard University Press, 2000), 485n1.

11. T. M. Scanlon, *What We Owe to Each Other* (Cambridge, MA: Harvard University Press, Belknap Press, 1998).
12. Ibid., 338.
13. Jürgen Habermas, *The Inclusion of the Other: Studies in Political Theory,* eds. Ciaran Cronin and Pablo De Greiff (Cambridge, MA: MIT Press, 1998), Chapter 1, 39.
14. Jürgen Habermas, *Moral Consciousness and Communicative Action,* trans. C. Lenhart and S. W. Nicholsen (Cambridge, MA: MIT Press, 1990), 197.
15. Habermas, *Inclusion of the Other,* 33.
16. Habermas, *Moral Consciousness,* 66.
17. Ibid., 68.
18. Scanlon, *What We Owe to Each Other,* 394.
19. Ibid., 343.
20. Habermas, *Inclusion of the Other,* 43.
21. Seyla Benhabib, *The Claims of Culture: Equality and Diversity in the Global Era* (Princeton and Oxford: Princeton University Press, 2002), 11.
22. Ibid., 12.
23. Alison Dundes Renteln, "A Cross-Cultural Approach to Validating International Human Rights: The Case of Retribution Tied to Proportionality," in *International Human Rights: Universalism versus Relativism* (Newbury Park, CA, and London: Sage, 1990), 88–137.
24. Ibid., 98, 100.
25. Ibid., 117.
26. David Daube, *Studies in Biblical Law* (New York: Ktav, 1969), 146, cited in Renteln, *International Human Rights,* 117. Renteln also cites similar claims by Hans Kelsen.
27. Renteln, *International Human Rights,* 118, 120.
28. Ibid., 126.
29. Ibid., 127, 130, 131.
30. Ibid., 130, 132.
31. Ibid., 135.
32. Ibid., 136–37.
33. Christine J. Walley, "Searching for 'Voices': Feminism, Anthropology, and the Global Debate over Female

Genital Operations," *Current Anthropology* 12, no. 3, 405–38.

34. Ibid., 411.

35. Ibid., 411–12.

36. Ibid.

37. For further discussion of these issues, see my book *Power: A Radical View*, 2nd ed. (London and New York: Palgrave Macmillan, 2005).

38. Bernard Williams, *Ethics and the Limits of Philosophy* (London: Fontana, 1985), 174.

39. Ibid., 6.

40. Ibid., 180.

41. Martha C. Nussbaum, *Women and Human Development: The Capabilities Approach* (Cambridge: Cambridge University Press, 2000), 69.

42. Ibid., 83.

43. Martha C. Nussbaum, *Frontiers of Justice: Disability, Nationality, Species Membership* (Cambridge, MA: Harvard University Press, Belknap Press, 2006), 70.

44. Ibid., 71.

45. Nussbaum, *Women and Human Development*, 101.

46. Nussbaum, *Frontiers of Justice*, 75.

47. Nussbaum, *Women and Human Development*, 81.

48. Ibid., Chapter 1.

49. Nussbaum, *Frontiers of Justice*, 78.

50. Ibid., 75.

51. Ibid., 78.

52. Nussbaum, *Women and Human Development*, 77.

53. Nussbaum, *Frontiers of Justice*, 78–79.

54. Nussbaum, *Women and Human Development*, 94.

55. Ibid., 74.

56. Ibid., 72.

57. Ibid., 99.

58. This suggested interpretation is also advanced by George Crowther in his interesting paper "Value Pluralism and Liberalism: Berlin and Beyond," in *The One and the Many: Reading Isaiah Berlin,* eds. George Crowther

and Henry Hardy (Amherst, NY: Prometheus Books, 2007), 207–30.

59. Ibid., 76.

60. Ibid., 83.

61. "Isaiah Berlin in Conversation with Steven Lukes," *Salmagundi,* no. 120 (Fall 1998), 119.

62. Isaiah Berlin, "My Intellectual Path," *New York Review of Books,* 14 May 1998, 57. For a fascinating discussion of what Berlin might have meant, see the Appendix by the editors to Crowther and Hardy, *The One and the Many*: "Berlin's Universal Values—Core or Horizon?" 293–97.

63. See my essay "Is Universalism Ethnocentric?" in Steven Lukes, *Liberals and Cannibals: The Implications of Diversity* (London: Verso, 2003) and Seyla Benhabib, "'Nous' et 'les Autres': The Politics of Complex Cultural Dialogue in a Global Civlization" in *Multicultural Questions,* eds. Christian Joppke and Steven Lukes (Oxford: Oxford University Press, 1999), reprinted in modified form in her *The Claims of Culture,* Chapter 2.

64. Sally Engle Merry, *Human Rights and Gender Violence: Translating International Law into Local Justice* (Chicago and London: Chicago University Press, 2006).

65. Ibid., 225–56.

66. Ibid., 226.

67. Ibid.

68. Ibid., 227.

69. Ibid.

70. Ibid., 25.

71. Brian Barry, *Culture and Equality: An Egalitarian Critique of Multiculturalism* (Cambridge: Polity, 2001), 262.

72. For evidence and discussion of such diversity within the United States alone, see *Handbook of Family Diversity,* eds. David H. Demo, Katherine R. Allen, and Mark A. Fine (New York: Oxford University Press, 1999).

SUGGESTIONS FOR FURTHER READING

Appiah, Kwame Anthony. *The Ethics of Identity*. Princeton and Oxford: Princeton University Press, 2005, new edition 2007.

Benhabib, Seyla. *The Claims of Culture: Equality and Diversity in the Global Era*. Princeton and Oxford: Princeton University Press, 2002.

Boudon, Raymond. *The Poverty of Relativism*. Oxford and Cambridge: Bardwell Press, 2004.

Cook, John W. *Morality and Cultural Differences*. New York: Oxford University Press, 1999.

Gellner, Ernest. *Postmodernism, Reason and Religion*. London and New York: Routledge, 1992.

Gowans, Christopher W. *Moral Disagreements: Classical and Contemporary Readings*. London and New York: Routledge, 2000.

Harman, Gilbert, and Judith Jarvis Thomson. *Moral Relativism and Moral Objectivity*. Oxford: Blackwell, 1996.

Hatch, Elvin. *Culture and Morality: The Relativity of Values in Anthropology*. New York: Columbia University Press, 1983.

Hauser, Marc D. *Moral Minds: How Nature Designed Our Universal Sense of Right and Wrong*. New York: Harper-Collins, 2006.

Hollis, Martin, and Steven Lukes, eds. *Rationality and Relativism*. Oxford: Blackwell; Cambridge, MA: MIT Press, 1982.

Levy, Neil. *Moral Relativism: A Short Introduction*. Oxford: Oneworld, 2002.

Meiland, Jack W., and Michael Krausz, eds. *Relativism: Cognitive and Moral*. Notre Dame, IN: Notre Dame University Press, 1982.

Midgley, Mary. *Can't We Make Moral Judgements?* New York: St. Martin's Press, 1991.

Moody-Adams, Michele M. *Fieldwork in Familiar Places: Morality, Culture, and Philosophy*. Cambridge, MA: Harvard University Press, 1997.

Moser, Paul K., and Thomas L. Carson, eds. *Moral Relativism: A Reader*. New York: Oxford University Press, 2001.

Renteln, Alison Dundes. *International Human Rights: Universalism versus Relativism*. Newbury Park, CA, and London: Sage, 1990.

Shweder, Richard. *Thinking Through Culture: Expeditions in Cultural Psychology*. Cambridge, MA: Harvard University Press, 1991.

Turiel, Eliot. *The Culture of Morality: Social Development, Context and Conflict*. Cambridge: Cambridge University Press, 2002.

Wallerstein, Immanuel. *European Universalism: The Rhetoric of Power*. New York: New Press, 2006.

Williams, Bernard. *Ethics and the Limits of Philosophy*. London: Fontana, 1985.

Wong, David B. *Moral Relativity*. Berkeley and Los Angeles: University of California Press, 1984.

ACKNOWLEDGMENTS

My warm thanks are due to the following persons for reading in whole or in part and commenting on earlier versions of this book: Gabriel Abend, Nicolas Baumard, Christopher Hann, Robin Marantz Henig, Amy Hong, Sally Merry, and Jennifer E. Telesca. I am grateful to them, even though I did not always take up their suggestions.

INDEX